— . —

The Astrological Cinema Ride

A Cosmic Take On Contemporary Cinema
B.P. Geiger

CONTENTS

—·—

INTRODUCTION

Gather around the fire, everyone. Have you ever heard of the extraordinary tale of when Mark Renton tried to avoid the scag, or when Luke was destined to become a Jedi? Or perhaps when Cady desired to be popular? The tales are among pop culture's most exciting. Mythology and its figures have influenced and continue to influence contemporary cinema. Much of the esoteric knowledge exhibited in this book is from the works of Santos Bonacci, Jordan Maxwell and Bill Donahue.

This book will interpret the astrological significance of the Hero's Journey and its comparison to the ancient zodiac by using six films as templates — *Star Wars: A New Hope* (1977), *Fear and Loathing in Las Vegas* (1998), *Superbad* (2007), *Trainspotting* (1996), *Mean Girls* (2004), and *Snatch* (2001).

The storylines pay homage to the movie gods while adhering to post-modern mythologies. And who are the movie gods? The Sun, the Moon, and the celestial rovers in the sky. The beloved sunlight is projected onto the silver screen of life, and we, the actors playing out each day, are indisputably prepped for our close-up!

Other writers have examined why the Hero's Journey is so powerful and fundamentally accepted worldwide. We will elaborate on this idea further by demonstrating the labyrinth of mythological references while looking at each film's many dimensional layers of astrological depth.

Within the Hero's Journey, the composition is a structure consistent with the laws of nature. The foundational aspects of the cosmos are demonstrated in front of our eyes, and we, as audience members, enjoy the rhythm that follows cosmic insight and esoteric philosophies. The path of the zodiac and the Hero's Journey, in which the microcosm reflects the macrocosm, serve as a lighthouse for elemental forces, perfectly expressing the Hermetic axiom *"As Above So Below, As Within So Without."*

The Hero's Journey is a tale about a tale that has influenced countless people's lives across several nations and eras. The narrative's core has yet to change and remains malleable, taking on many different forms. A hero learns skills ideal for the difficulties of setting out on an initiation; they experience the nuances of a "special world" and resolve with a return.

The Hero With A Thousand Faces, written by mythologist and author Joseph Campbell in 1949, captures the traditional Hero's Journey story framework and shows how the archetypal hero develops throughout history in myths and tales that all people share. Christopher Vogler, a Hollywood development executive, and author, published *The Writer's Journey* in the early 1990s, furthering Joseph Campbell's theory and organizing the many sub-steps of the Hero's Journey into twelve separate stages.

Joseph Campbell and Christopher Vogler exemplify this endeavor by depicting the journey as a circle with a line through it. This form implies the need to return to the starting place as a newly developed character, similar to how the Sun participates in the annual passage contained within a closed system as two halves create a whole.

Like the names of stars, constellation names come from various sources, each with a unique origin and meaning. The genesis of many myths and legends throughout history can be found in the constellations and the number of zodiac signs. *The Clash of the Twelve Titans, The Story of the Twelve Disciples, The Twelve Labors of Hercules,* and *The Legend of King Arthur* are examples.

The Sun is the epitome of the hero on the quest embarking on a prevailing campaign in character form. They are interchangeable. The Sun's constant passage through the sky and the classic depiction of the hero reflect a single focal point exhibiting duality along a twelve-layered pilgrimage.

Since the Hero's Journey is a symbolic representation of the omnipresent wanderer, it is adored and cherished worldwide. Once the connection is made, the similarities between astrology and the Hero's Journey become strikingly clear. Both follow a "hero" departing on a voyage evoking psychological and prolific emotional catharsis.

The film's plot, the Hero's Journey map, and the Sun's progression through the zodiac are all combined into a single symbolic personification. Minor characters along the route give the adventure's many archetypes form as it progresses from **The Ordinary World** to **Return With the Elixir**.

Some people would argue that the predestined journey of the hero pigeonholes creativity. Yet, Campbell expertly shows how this pattern cuts through numerous cultures and historical periods, demonstrating that the hero appears in varying faces. The idea of a myriad of masks is also expressed in astrology since a birth chart has countless astrological configurations.

The Hero's Journey's overarching trajectory and the zodiac signs depict the basic flow of matter shifting between electricity (masculine) and magnetism (feminine). Masculine and feminine energy does not strictly refer to man's or woman's attributes but to the everlasting balancing of polarity within nature.

In astrology, the twelve signs represent energy delivery that oscillates between opposites. An external push of motion is represented by electricity or "masculine" potency, while an interior pull is represented by magnetism or "feminine" power. The Sun's path through the astrological wheel can be described as an "in breath" and an "out breath." The hero will experience the two opposing sides as they enter each stage, riding the repeating myth's locomotion as it swings back and forth.

Aries is electric, male, and Yang. **Taurus** is magnetic, feminine, and Yin. **Gemini** is electric, masculine, Yang, etc. The twin principles of conscious and subconscious, hot and cold, day and night, Yin and Yang, masculine and feminine, alternate as the structural arrangement.

A rhythmic flow through the elements starts in fire, then earth, air, and ends in water. Fire and air continuously unfurl electricity, while earth and water characterize magnetism.

Fire is considered spirit released outward, earth is physical expression planted inward, air is the activation of thought outward, and water symbolizes internal feelings. Spirit, physicality, thought, and emotional imagination are the fourfold nature of the elements at play. This progression will manifest three times throughout the astrological wheel.

Aside from the Sun and Moon, the other visible luminaries inhabit duality within two zodiac signs. Mercury is the planetary ruler of both **Virgo** and **Gemini** and embodies electricity in **Gemini** and magnetism in **Virgo**. Venus is electrically charged in **Libra** and magnetically potent in **Taurus**. Mars is electric in **Aries** and magnetic in **Scorpio**.

Jupiter rules over masculine **Sagittarius** and feminine **Pisces**. Saturn coordinates magnetic **Capricorn** and electric **Aquarius**.

The heroes display the duality of reality within the electromagnetic realm by partaking in the voyage through the ecliptic belt and depicting the attributes of each step of the Hero's Journey. As the main characters transition into the new zodiac stage, they will form traits of that particular sign, similar to the Sun's yearly passing through each astrological sign.

The Hero's Journey archetypes are distinct from those of the zodiac. The archetypes on the hero's path assist the larger goal and are carefully used not to overpower the narrative. We will discuss how astrological archetypes can manifest and symbolize the subtleties of each sign, as well as how they might be embodied as archetypes within the Hero's Journey. The astrological signs function similarly to the specific archetypes in Campbell's work as distinct stepping stones; however, they are more prominently displayed at each stage in this book.

Although it is unnecessary, watching each movie again can be beneficial beforehand, after, or both. We are viewing the film via an astrological prism. After using this analytical technique, you will be able to see for yourself the information offered. The experience of watching a movie can vary every time.

Another critical point to mention is that this book discusses tropical astrology. The Sun's position along the ecliptic belt remains unwavering. The Sun moves through twelve phases, thematically expressing psychological states of being, yet its location and motion are constant yearly.

The Sun and the hero undergo the majestic stages as they travel on an anchored rail line that twists, dips, and surprises along the way. So grab a seat, butter some popcorn, and prepare for *The Astrological*

Cinema Ride. The dramatic departure melts the ice in the element of fire.

1

---·---

ARIES - THE ORDINARY WORLD

F rom darkness, the first breath of life inhales and then exhales. A
 dim spark of brilliance fades in. In Aries, the astrological new
year commences at the spring equinox spearheading a fresh start and
a strong desire to begin a new day. Propelling momentum like a bat-
tering ram rupturing the fall of night, the glittering glory of the rising
Sun kick starts the epic quest by eradicating the void of empty space.

Aries brings to view the portal from which we emerged—the birth
of consciousness through the birth canal. The glyph for Aries fluctu-
ates between the ram's horns and the womb simultaneously. The ram's
horn stands for when the seed of consciousness is urged to leave the
womb; the only way to go is brazenly forward.

One of the most well-known constellations in the starry night
sky near Aries is Perseus and Medusa. This constellation and famous
Greek myth depicts the young warrior Perseus dispatched to his alleged death to kill the gorgon Medusa. Thanks to Athena and Hermes'
assistance, he survives and chops off Medusa's head while concurrently
saving Princess Andromeda from a sea monster.

This story in the stars correlates with Aries being the warrior sign of
the zodiac that symbolically slashes the head of darkness and liberates
the arrival of the divine feminine. The warrior's appearance ushers in a

new dawn and blazes the trail for the other zodiac signs. The journey's first stage encourages visual delight, ridiculous dialogue, and direct action in introducing **The Ordinary World**.

Star Wars: A New Hope

As the title suggests, a conflict in the stars activates George Lucas's epic cinematic story. **The Ordinary World** opens with an enormous Empire battleship hovering overhead and shooting at another spaceship, grabbing the audience's attention with action.

The film cuts to inside the smaller spaceship, and the two droids, C3-PO and R2-D2, appear to face certain death. Aries ignites the journey and the rebirth of light through stylized and occasional absolute destruction. An explosion on the spacecraft introduces the main antagonist Darth Vader.

One half of the hero archetype, Princess Leia, symbolically portrays the mythical notion of the Virgin Mary. She gives birth to a new consciousness and disperses a flicker of new hope. She successfully provides the droid R2-D2 with crucial information for the Rebel Alliance. This represents Mother Mary's virgin birth on a symbolic level. Princess Leia embodies the Moon as the feminine half of the hero archetype.

As we will see in most of the movies discussed in this book, the hero occasionally serves as two characters. The personification of the Sun will play the electrical masculine leading role in the journey, and the other leading role, embodiment of the feminine magnetic aspect of the archetypal hero, personifies the Moon. The hero is periodically divided into two, paying homage to the solar and lunar heavenly bodies.

The ominous Darth Vader takes the princess prisoner, but R2-D2 and C3-PO launch out of a pod and barely escape the Empire's grasp.

The two droids land on the scorching and desolate planet "Tatooine." They argue about which direction to go and split up.

While adhering to the themes of Aries, the two are establishing a future for themselves and asserting one's individuality. They roam the planet separately. R2-D2 and C3-PO eventually cross paths again as they are captured by "Jawas." These little nefarious characters can be representative of Aries themes as they assert dominance over the terrain.

The electrical archetypal hero, Luke Skywalker, is introduced at the end of the Aries section. As Santos Bonacci and Jordan Maxwell have said, this iconic character represents the Sun walking the stars. R2 and C3-PO ultimately join Luke on the Hero's Journey quest.

Fear and Loathing in Las Vegas

Aries awakens in a red Chevrolet Impala, driving through the Nevada desert; inside are Hunter S. Thompson and his attorney Dr. Gonzo. These two hero archetypes embark on a savage hallucinogenic adventure into the core of the American dream. Thompson embodies the helios hero as the Sun and Dr. Gonzo as the celestial Moon.

Within the first few minutes, **The Ordinary World** is depicted, and the way of life of these mischievous characters is presented. Hunter pulls over the car and opens the trunk to uncover many mind-altering psychedelics. In narration, he points out that although they do not require much, he often pushes things as far as possible. Aries, the great pioneer of the zodiac, urges the hero to take action first and ask questions later. The first sign begins the initiation process without knowing how to finish it.

Following the opening scene, the heroes pick up a hitchhiker and instruct him to enter without hesitation. The heroes wait until the hitchhiker is comfortably settled in the backseat before inquiring about his plans. Thompson displays Aries' resolve to move forward by mentally navigating any obstacles.

Potential risks are listed by Hunter's internal voice-over, which indicates unlikely and malicious consequences. Will they need to do this before completing that? Deductive reasoning always heralds an imprint into the landscape for the fearless champion of the astrological wheel.

Superbad

Seth drives to pick up his closest buddy Evan for their final high school days in the opening scene of the coming-of-age movie *Superbad*. Seth is the hero giving form to the Solar energy, and Evan is the magnetic Lunar embodiment.

The first sign symbolically corresponds to the infancy stages if the complete zodiac is compared to the lifespan of a human being. When an infant is born, the naming process begins, planting a map displaying a label for all to recognize.

Seth recommends research over the phone for when they both start college the following year. Seth tells Evan that he found the optimal website to subscribe to, "The Vagtastic Voyage." With a touch of humor, this is a nod to the birthing process when the soul enters the body through the female reproductive system.

The solar and lunar archetypes merge when Seth gets to Evan's house. As Evan's mother enters the scene, Seth is seen gazing at her breasts. He tells Evan he would like to suckle on her breast like an infant would.

The heroes then go to a nearby convenience store. In a conversation, Seth refers to the tendency of Aries to push the envelope to exhaustion.

Seth mentions how the famous Orson Welles ate himself to death and makes a veiled allusion to how enthusiasm might push the boundaries of potentiality too far.

An encounter with a high school bully who fits the aggressive side of martial Aries occurs as Seth and Evan leave the store. Violence could have resulted from this; however, these heroes are not the typical violent breed.

In the following scene, Evan further establishes the theme of exaggeration and explains **The Ordinary World** by broadening the scope of his regular Friday nights to his ideal female counterpart Becca. During the cutaway flashback scenes, the audience is made aware of the falsity of his narration.

Seth is seen running laps in gym class as the Aries portion draws to a close. Showing exhaustion, he presents the necessity to slow down in the final degrees of strong-willed Aries.

Trainspotting

Cross-examining the first scene of *Trainspotting*, Aries features the characters running straight ahead. A voice-over recounts what to choose from life's endless possibilities. The hero is making the first move and has a solid desire immediately.

As the story progresses, a montage of the main characters' copious activities is edited together in quick cuts. The names of the major players are listed and displayed on screen. This montage illustrates the reality and self-image of the main characters within their environment.

Cutting to a soccer/futbol match, the ball strikes Mark Renton, the quest's main character, the lone hero, and the Sun's manifestation in character form. Renton is played by Aries Sun sign Ewan McGregor. He receives a direct blow to the forehead from the ball. This corresponds to Aries governing the top of the human body and the prefrontal cortex, also known as the cerebrum. After completing his narration, Renton states that every action is perpetually followed by a calculated choice based on an initial impulse.

Mean Girls

In *Mean Girls*, the spark of consciousness is reborn as two parents stare into the camera in the opening shot, akin to a child's perspective from a crib. Cut to a broad perspective to see Cady, the hero embarking on the journey toward self-individuation. Her parents are sending her off to her first day of high school. Cady explains in narration that they recently came from Africa to America — a reference to the idea that Africa is a cradle of human civilization.

Cady enrolls in her first class and is introduced to the principal Mr. Duvall and math teacher Ms. Norbury. These archetypes stand for the complementary nature of reality as it is expressed as masculine and feminine or electricity and magnetism.

Cady becomes familiar with this new world, and the film eventually shows her eating an apple all by her lonesome in a bathroom stall. The hero is unquestionably unfamiliar with this new environment during the early stage and showcases a depiction of the biblical Garden of Eden. A torus field is an energetic sacred geometric composition that resembles an apple in appearance and is considered to be the shape of the active human body. Biting into the apple in the Garden of Eden is a symbolic rendering of the transition of spirit into matter during the incarnation in human form.

On her second day, Cady encounters Janis and Damian, two misfits, and they skip class together and sit outside. The film further familiarizes Cady's likeness and the other primary characters. Gretchen

Wieners, Karen Smith, and Regina George, known as the "Plastics," enter the location as Janice and Damien narrate their story to Cady. Cue the Missy Elliot music!

The Plastics stand in for the Sun on the astrological wheel as the cardinal points. The signs Aries, Cancer, Libra, and Capricorn form a cross known as "The Royal Grand Cross," also known as "The Four Horsemen of the Apocalypse." The four cardinal points in astrology and "The Four Horsemen of the Apocalypse" in the Bible can be tied to the Plastics as unquestionably those who will conquer the hearts and minds of individuals in the school.

Ramming Regina George, regarded as exalted at this time, has a fiery temperament adapted to the Sun's position in Aries. Karen, who is mysterious and claims to have psychic skills, mimics the Sun in Cancer. Gretchen Wieners strikes a chord with the Sun in Capricorn and is a skilled observer of the rules. And Cady completes the cross as the Libra archetype since she contrasts Regina George's personality and has a harmonious bond with others.

The audience gets a sense of staging when the film shifts to the cafeteria and establishes **The Ordinary World**. Cady receives a map from Janis showing the locations of each clique.

Snatch

Snatch introduces Turkish and Tommy as the significant hero figures in the film. Turkish portrays the light of day, and Tommy is the magnetic orb of night. The other ensemble cast members are astrological stereotypes sprinkled in along the way. Turkish articulates in the voice-over that he and Tommy promote boxing in London.

The personification of the Aries Sun, Franky Four Fingers, ignites **The Ordinary World**. Before a diamond heist, Franky and three other robbers dressed as stereotypical Jewish men stroll through an office building in Antwerp.

A symbol of purity, eternity, and unstoppable spiritual strength, the diamond is the Sun's talisman, not as a person but as a physical object. The ownership of the diamond is directly related to the Sun's position in a specific zodiac sign and in the hands of a particular astrological figure, as is further illustrated throughout the plot.

The security camera tracks these men and acts as the audience's point of view. As these men are calmly going about their business before an explosion of violence, the setting humorously heightens the suspense. The film begins in black and white while the security cameras track these characters, but everything changes to color once they enter the office. The difference between monochrome and color visually imitates being birthed into the world of visible light.

An explosion of fast-paced jump cuts and music signals the start of the diamond robbery and explicitly conveys the surge of tenacious vigor. There are audible cues of shouting and argument as the fury of Aries intensifies before Franky gets his hands on the diamond. The Aries archetype is shown as holding dominion over the Sun since he now owns the diamond.

The film then turns to the intro of the other key cast members in montage-style graphics as their names and images appear, further establishing **The Ordinary World**. After the heist, the Aries section finalizes as one of the other robbers tells Franky to contact Boris "The Blade" if he needs a gun when he arrives in London. Boris will characterize the opposing side as the Libra archetype.

2

— • —

TAURUS - THE CALL TO ADVENTURE

Forward masculine impulse from Aries arising and asserting sovereignty in all its glory slows down in Taurus's earthy feminine magnetic polarity. Aries leads the way with an electrical charge to clear the path, and stillness and silence, which never ends, arrives second to receive.

It is time to concentrate on what occurs after establishing individuality. The hero is called out of **The Ordinary World** using their unique potential while the forward trajectory puts on the breaks. **The Call to Adventure** seems like something the hero could only credibly fathom doing. This is their destiny drawing near.

The Call to Adventure displays how the mission is presented. However, only the call is made apparent— not the acceptance of it. Later, in the next magnetic feminine sign, that will happen. Taurus is a fixed earth sign that encourages anchoring one's feet firmly in place and drawing from within.

The electrical realm is outward and temporal; because of this, electrical devices require recharging after an initial power surge. On the other side, magnetism is constant and unchanging.

The second sign of the zodiac is associated with the mythology of the Minotaur. Bull worship has been practiced throughout history in

various ways, in a literal and a mythological sense. Honoring magnetism can be compared to worshiping the bull.

The hero will gain steadiness to be launched into the unfolding
mission upfront by maintaining composure. As a result, the focus
shifts from *what* one is doing to *how* one is doing it. This is a restoration phase where developing inner principles are presented as the bull
picks up the blazing baton of the Sun.

Star Wars: A New Hope

After the forcefulness of Aries has subsided, C3-PO receives a
much-needed oil bath. The audience acquires an understanding of this
character's capabilities and code of ethics as the helpful mechanical
device introduces himself to Luke. Venus, the planetary ruler of Taurus, draws attention to the construction of C3-PO's physical body.

It should be mentioned that bronze is used in the droid's plating;
however, because it has a similar color and texture to copper, the
plating can be compared visually and astrologically reminiscent of the
metal linked with Venus. In addition, C3-PO is compared to Venus'
characteristics since he displays a wide range of perceptivity. While
R2-D2 is opposed in nature and features, the droid is comparable to
Mars's ideologies as a force for progress.

Luke receives **The Call to Adventure** as a message appears from
R2-D2. Princess Leia again displays the magnetic polarity of the hero
archetype and communicates her need for assistance from "Obi-Wan
Kenobi." She sets up the path ahead for the Sun. Still, Luke has yet to
embrace the call.

Young Skywalker, unable to understand **The Call to Adventure**,
has dinner with Uncle Owen and Aunt Beru, two Taurus archetypes.
When Luke brings up the message, Uncle Owen, sternly like a bull,

tells his nephew to ignore it to protect him indirectly. Although Luke storms off disappointed, he has an innate sense that he is intended for something, even though he is not entirely conscious of his possible calling.

Luke's resemblance to his father is openly mentioned by Aunt Beru, who portrays the opposing side of the Taurus archetype and offers a grounded viewpoint. Here, Luke's value is highlighted, and the viewer is shown the possibility of the hero's call to destiny.

Fear and Loathing in Las Vegas

In the backseat with the hitchhiker, Thompson describes how he obtained the convertible to get to where he is now. The hero appraises the work that has been done. The film cuts back to the previous few days.

Hunter Thompson and Dr. Gonzo enjoy Singapore slings at The Beverly Hills Hotel's Polo Lounge. Venus implores the soul to pause and enjoy the blossoms. A tracking shot introducing **The Call to Adventure** follows a waiter holding a phone through the hotel lobby before arriving on Hunter and Dr. Gonzo to deliver a literal call to the hero. Hunter is given the opportunity to participate in "The Mint 400" motocross race in the Las Vegas desert as a journalist.

Dr. Gonzo lists the physical requirements for the journey in detail and shows examples of artifacts that demonstrate the element of fixed earth—Taurus signals material objects as a direct reflection of one's moral code. Fashion and the items in one's environment are ways to exhibit one's taste.

As Gonzo and Thompson leave the Pogo Lounge, Thompson says they must do it right if they choose to take up the call. Because Taurus moves slowly and steadily, a commitment is fulfilled with constant attention and adequate accuracy.

The flashback ends with the two heroes gathering goods from various locations in Los Angeles and purchasing the car from the dealership to flee into the present moment.

Superbad

The second stage of Taurus, equivalent to nurturing physicality, takes hold in home economics class. Ms. Hayworth, the teacher, is rooted in her beliefs and plays the role of a stereotypical Taurus. She listens calmly while Seth laments the lack of a cooking companion or his "other half." Aries' electrical vitality necessitates its magnetic complement. Realistically, Ms. Hayworth acknowledges that she did not create odd numbers.

The first even sign is linked to the biblical character "Eve." This prompts the introduction of Jules, Seth's new culinary companion. In a montage, Seth (Adam) and Jules (Eve) collaborate to produce tiramisu in the Garden of Eden. When Seth receives **The Call to Adventure**, he is filled with joy. The hero is invited to Jules' end-of-year graduation party.

Trainspotting

In the fixed modality of Taurus, Renton decides to take a step back from his aggressive pace and assign reverence by quitting heroin. There is a shot of Renton nailing the door to his flat from the inside; he narrates how he exercises self-control. He lists tangible items for the call: tranquil music, ice cream, vitamins, etc. The hero needs an extra push because this **Call to Adventure** is tricky, and Renton still needs to fully engross himself in the call.

Cut to Renton buying opium suppositories from Mikey Forrester, a Taurus archetype. Mikey says he has suppositories specially designed for progressive release, which parallels the Sun's movement from Aries to Taurus. The suppositories are ingested obstinately by Renton, who continues his day.

The hero's need for release suddenly hits him, and the film eventually shows him at the most grotesque toilet in Scotland. A surrealistic scene occurs there as he fornicates his suppositories. Renton falls headfirst into the toilet outlandishly and lands in a sizeable body of water.

He sinks to the bottom of the deep, blue sea, retrieves his fluorescent suppositories, and then floats back to the surface. The lower portion of the brain, which corresponds to the subconscious, is depicted here visually.

As mentioned in the previous chapter, the cerebrum is related to Aries, the front part of the brain, and the conscious mind. The sign of the bull is linked to the cerebellum, the bottom portion of the brain, and the subconscious mind. The zodiac's first two signs suggest the formation of physical consciousness inside the head. This is why the film shows an abstract scene that winks at the subliminal mind.

Mean Girls

In the girls' bathroom, the second stage of the quest begins as Cady tells Janice and Damian that Ramming Regina showed a liking toward her. Janis suggests **The Call to Adventure** for the hero to infiltrate the Plastics and destroy them from within. Cady, though, waits to grow emotionally committed before accepting her summons.

Aaron Samuels, the hero's primary love interest, enters the picture as the divine male counterpart. He serves as Cady's internal **Call to Adventure** and is comparable to the mythical Taurus golden calf. Cady mentions how her infatuation wallops her like a bus. (Nice foreshadowing, Tina Fey!)

Snatch

There is a need for restoration for the primary characters as the transition from fiery Aries to receptive Taurus begins. Turkish and Tommy speak about the need for a new caravan in which to live. Turkish claims that a gypsy camp can provide them with a new one. This small **Call to Adventure** will trigger events, setting the course for the rest of the journey.

The primary **Call to Adventure** for Turkish and Tommy is delivered by the main antagonist and Taurus archetype Brick Top at his pig farm. Brick Top is a solid force to be reckoned with, giving the heroes a sense of material and personal possessions.

Brick Top intends to utilize Turkish's fighter Gorgeous George as a combatant in a rigged boxing match that will take place in a few days. Taurus is associated with defining a set of personal beliefs; thus, Turkish makes reference in the voice-over to how it is challenging enough to make a career in the boxing business, and occasionally you have to act contrary to your predetermined principles.

3

GEMINI - REFUSAL OF THE CALL

A focal point materializes a reflection to be placed on a newly born human avatar. This process began in Aries and was valued in Taurus. **Refusal of the Call** follows **The Call to Adventure** as a potential gain or loss from the journey. The idea of existing in a world of opposites — such as good and evil, angels and demons, left and right, day and night, hot and cold, electric and magnetic — comes into sharp focus as the thematic backdrop of the twins of Gemini.

Between two opposing forces, there is a delicate middle ground. The third-dimensional realm is a combination of opposites existing in the spectrum of the mind. Two halves of the mind create a conscious driving force that expresses manifested reality.

The third stage emphasizes the knowledge that one's interactions with others only reflect one's psychological state. This idea shapes the hero's highly individual vision and illustrates other people's perspectives within a community. The hero is interested in others while challenging their eccentric viewpoint. Usually, two characters discuss **The Call to Adventure** while deliberating between two possible courses of action.

The electrical Yang archetype swings back in and implores the ability to juggle two points of view at once. The merger of the two sides into one is why the luminary that rules Gemini is considered androgynous. A third is created by the first two elements working together.

We may not physically see the wind, but we can hear it as Gemini has the gift of gab. The concept of thought and mental cognition is associated with airflow. The wind and the first air sign of the zodiac are expressed via mutability, which is particularly unpredictable since it can move in any direction. Gemini enables the hero, who now has a sense of self, to communicate that self through speech and cognitive reasoning.

The term "trickster" is associated with Gemini and refers to the self-hood that acts most of the time and is comparable to the human being living existence by simultaneously accepting life as a finite mortal and infinite source essence. People are paradoxes in motion.

The glass is always half full and half empty. It only depends on your point of view whether you choose to concentrate on the apparent good or the bad. The choice is yours.

Star Wars: A New Hope

As **Refusal of the Call** gets going, Luke and C3-PO look for R2-D2, who left the previous night. The heroes keep the plot moving while subtly carrying out the objective of discovering Obi-Wan Kenobi. R2-D2 is eventually located, but "Tusken Raiders" ambush Luke. The Raiders are characterized as Gemini representations and the idea of mercurial air. They are a nomadic clan, and their voice performs a wide range of pitches, adding to an ominous and frightening sense of danger.

This moment sufficiently startles Skywalker as he is almost captured. For the Gemini hero, the current circumstances can go either way. Unpredictability returns as a hooded figure materializes. Another acoustic defense rings out and disperses the cause of the alarm. Luke is given a break.

Ben Kenobi, an old friend of young Skywalker, is there as he awakens. He informs Ben of R2-D2's message about an "Obi-Wan." Thematically, identity is portrayed in this dual sign, and Ben exposes himself to be Obi-Wan Kenobi. He is demonstrating two personalities that exist simultaneously.

Obi-Wan is considered the mentor archetype in this film's overall Hero's Journey layout; however, this iconic character also plays as a Gemini archetype according to *The Astrological Cinema Ride*.

So think of it like Obi-Wan is a mentor with a Gemini flare. Also, he is introduced during this stage before the fourth stage because he is being set up for the mentor's meeting. If he arrived during **Meeting With the Mentor**, it would be too much to fit in before the wise guide could deliver the necessary troupes to the story.

Fear and Loathing in Las Vegas

As the Impala pulls over and the hitchhiker flees after getting spooked by the mindless babble Hunter and Gonzo spew out, the Gemini stage begins, and a sense of humor enters. The incident amuses Gonzo and Hunter, who continue their journey to Las Vegas.

The protagonist moves into the third stage, **Refusal of the Call**, anticipating all consequences and any potentialities. At this level of growth, the protagonist asks, "Who am I?" Hunter Thompson also goes by the fictitious name "Raul Duke." Gonzo asks Hunter whether he's prepared to check into a hotel using a false name. The heroes embrace unpredictability, taking some of the "sunshine acid" while traveling at high speed thirty minutes before Vegas.

The acid takes effect when the two arrive on the strip. Waiting in line to check into his hotel room, Hunter (or Raul Duke) notices a nearby person conversing on the phone, visually demonstrating the element of air traveling the airwaves.

The heroes manage to enter the hotel bar, and as Hunter flows in, he sees his reflection in a mirror and unmistakably puts onto display the twins of Gemini. Is he Raul Duke or Hunter Thompson? He's both.

When the acid finally reaches its zenith, enormous lizards drinking alcohol and partaking in an orgy in the bar suddenly appear. This prominent scene acknowledges the boundaries of rational reasoning and conscious perception reaching an apex.

The fight-or-flight mode in the brain is dealt with by the "reptilian mind," which is the ego's conscious awareness to keep one alive. The human psyche can feel like a complex web due to the many cognizant channels, and it can be challenging to look beyond the boundaries of conventional comprehension in the final degrees of inquisitive Gemini.

Superbad

The third stage of the wheel takes shape, prompting the introduction of the third leading presence, Fogell. He illustrates creating a mental avatar placed upon a freshly born conscious awareness. He informs Seth and Evan of his plans to buy a false ID later that day. Fogell is the Gemini archetype or "shapeshifter," as he will soon accept his dual disposition.

After class, Seth embraces Gemini's flexibility and agrees to purchase booze for Jules and her party. He naively and courteously accepts her offer. Cut to Seth suggesting to Evan that if they obtain an assemblage of alcohol for Jules using Fogell's ID, ultimately, this will result in losing their virginity. Evan muses about temperamental outcomes and dispenses potential unpredictability as he alludes to a **Refusal of the Call**. Despite these possibilities, Seth persuades Evan of his clever scheme.

After becoming persuaded by Mercury's reasoning skills, Evan also offers to buy a bottle of "Goldslick Vodka" for Becca. Something that will have a direct callback in Gemini's opposite sign Sagittarius.

Fogell reappears with his fake ID, which he shows to Seth and Evan. The information presented on the ID is one name and a birth date that falls in the Gemini season on June 3, 1982. Seth and Evan are dubious and suggest another **Refusal of the Call** since outlooks can contain erratic changeability. Evan proposes the choice is ultimately up to Fogell and upholds the theme of choosing a perspective.

Fogell then welcomes the dichotomy of the twins and boldly claims to be "McLovin." The Gemini stage comes to a close with Seth lost in the act of a nearly-graduated senior having his car towed for parking in a teacher's spot.

Trainspotting

Mark Renton describes in narration his continual attempt and struggles to avoid the scag as **Refusal of the Call** arrives. The hero encounters one of his friends, the character Sick Boy in a park. The two visually appear similar to The Lovers card in the Tarot and the two halves of the brain.

Renton claims he can hardly look at his friends because they remind him so much of himself. The hero's inner self is mirrored in the other characters. Sick Boy is regarded as embodying a Gemini archetype. He is imitating Renton's behavior and quitting heroin because he is experimenting with his perspective on life instead of doing it out of obligation.

Cut to the two shooting pedestrians with a BB gun. Gemini expresses a particular verbal philosophy, which inspires Sick Boy to share his overarching perspective of life. According to his theory, everyone moves upward in life before suddenly moving downward and unquestionably deducting duality woven into the fabric of reality. You can be hot one moment and not the next.

As Renton ends the scene and narrates that he must somehow integrate into society, Gemini is an example of various viewpoints forming a populace. He emphasizes the necessity of establishing locality and sustaining coexistence.

The film cuts to the other prominent figures who live in the cinematic universe. We witness a montage of Begbie, Tommy, and Spud. They are considered various expressions of Renton's psyche and the multiple pieces of Scotland's psychological adolescence. These supporting players depict Gemini's astrological characteristics in the context of the neighborhood where the protagonist lives.

Begie is a raving lunatic who draws energy from his violent wolfish side. Tommy describes to Renton a flashback in which Begbie assaults another player while playing a game of pool. In contrast to Begbie, Tommy is more forgiving and has a positive outlook on life. These opposites are introduced to demonstrate the idea of an imbalance between opposing natures. Begbie and Tommy can not play the dual essence of Germini since they lean too much in one direction.

Spud represents the adaptable character of Gemini's mutability and is another aspect of Renton's mentality: mutable air releases thoughts and speech quickly while dissolving in miscellaneous ways. Spud is seen going through a job interview on speed, and his mercurial mind babbles.

Mean Girls

Cady senses the urge for communication with her male consort and the golden calf, Aaron Samuels, at the start of the Gemini stage. This serves as a potential threat to her **Call to Adventure** and suggests a **Refusal of the Call**. In Gemini, an articulation inside a coherent syndicate unravels as the film cuts to Cady and the Plastics in the cafeteria.

Regina exits stage right as the dialogue progresses, and Cady tells Gretchen about her new crush. Gretchen asserts that Aaron Samuels is Regina's ex-boyfriend and is categorically off-limits while adhering to the ideology of feminism. The film then cuts to promote one of the many clubs that Cady might join within this new community known as "The Mathletes."

The following scene illustrates Gemini's theme of opposing viewpoints presented through a linguistic exhibition. When Regina approaches Cady in her convertible, she uses a snarky double entendre that refers to Cady as a loser while carrying a kernel of truth.

Cady and the Plastics go shopping at the mall, and Cady narrates in voice-over how she sees similarities between people walking around the mall and animals at a watering hole. She relays the idea of oscillating between the notion that one can live with personal autonomy or follow the herd.

When the film cuts to Regina's home, her mother is introduced. She expresses yet another dual Gemini concept. She describes herself as a trendy mom instead of a typical one. Regina's mom distributes drinks as a treat for "hump day." The seven visible luminaries in the sky align with the seven days of the week. The ruler of Gemini, Mercury, corresponds to Wednesday, also known as "hump day."

The provocative "Burn Book" is revealed as the Gemini portion continues. This is a literary tool that the Plastics created comprised of pages holding all the school's pupils' secrets. The element of malleable air fuels scandal and greases the wheels of rumors. This book serves as a tool that personifies a method of following a set of idealized rules. Gemini governs the double hands, which help the brain to reflect and put the ideas of spirit into words.

The god Thoth from ancient Egypt exhibits traits similar to Mercury and the term "thought." Thoth takes over the function of the timekeeper and is shown clutching a scroll known as "The Book of Records." The Burn Book and Thoth's Book of Records represent a materialization of the different qualities of the intellect in a tangible object.

In the next scene, the film depicts Cady engaging in her first "3-way phone attack!" Gemini ideals act as information agents enacted across the airwaves. The conversation is shown on a split-screen, which underlines Gemini's principles of verbally providing information within a dual framework. Regina claims to be aware of Cady's crush on the golden calf.

The refusal stage culminates during math class, and Aaron invites Cady to a costume Halloween party. The two lovers' synergy incorporates a symbiosis in the latter degrees of the twins.

Snatch

During a split-screen phone call with his brother, Boris The Blade opens the Gemini section, which visually evokes the two halves of the brain and the twins of Gemini. As word spreads over the airwaves about the diamond and Franky Four Fingers' terrible gambling addiction, the mercurial facts set a plan into motion. It is established that

Boris, who plays the Libra archetype in this movie, is out to get his opposite, the Aries archetype, Franky Four Fingers. Libra intends to steal the diamond (the Sun).

The constellations Castor and Pollux are connected to the sign of Gemini. These two celestial twin beings stand for the twins' heads compared to Boris and his brother. In Greek mythology, Castor and Pollux were identical twins, with Pollux being the brighter of the two stars. Gemini and Mercury are metaphorically categorized as cunning "tricksters" since the essential nature of duality is fundamentally contradictory.

Another Gemini embodiment is introduced as Avi, the American living in New York City. He is seen on the phone with Franky, who is getting tailored for a suit in London. In a back-and-forth phone sequence, Franky tells Avi about his ownership of the diamond and plans to sell it to him. Franky's attire changes as the film cuts between the two, suggesting unpredictability and the shedding of a range of masks or personas.

A diamond store owner Doug "The Head" is another Gemini stereotype. Doug illustrates the idea of a second persona as the owner of a diamond store who, for professional reasons, poses as being Jewish.

As the camera tracks Doug on the phone, he enters his shop, and his twin daughters appear behind the counter. This is heavily laying the visual foundation of the twins of Gemini.

When the final part of **Refusal of the Call** manifests, Franky Four Fingers purchases a revolver from the trickster and his opposite, Boris The Blade. If Franky places a bet for Boris at a bookie for an illegal boxing match, he will give the gun to Franky for free.

Boris then suggests a twofold interpretation and sows the seed of deception. He claims to know information that Franky does not.

Franky believes Boris is talking about the result of the boxing match that is fixed, but he is subtly claiming he is aware of the diamond. Mr. Four Fingers agrees to place the bet and indicates losing control of his more frivolous side. There is an imbalance between the two halves of Franky.

4

— . —

CANCER - MEETING WITH THE MENTOR

I t is revealed in this step that **The Call to Adventure** is a retelling of a particular ancient rhythm of destiny, showing that the hero's circumstances are not senseless acts of random happenings. Past archetypal heroes who bravely undertook this voyage in their own time and manner have already existed.

The heroes partake in the **Meeting With the Mentor** and gather a dated toolkit to gain access to transcendental cognition. The traditional mentor provides the hero with security, whether a person, a tangible object, or some informational data. The mentor presents the idea that the subject of the quest has deeper origins.

The time has come for the hero to answer the call of antiquity and bring something unique to the mission. They recognize the vastness of their special calling that leads to their ultimate fate. On a distinct emotional and purely subjective level, the calling is validated. The hero will experience sensory delight while opening the floodgates to their creative powers as they visualize their perfect version and deeply bury into the safety of a solid self-identity.

The Moon, the moderator of enchantment and the ruler of the mystical fourth sign, details the many emotional ebbs and flows of the human body and mind. The Moon's everchanging face has been allegorically connected to the idea of artful "deceit." This is not meant to be taken literally; it is only an allusion to the unfailing variability of the lunar surface, unlike the Sun, which never waxes or wanes but only shifts its position on the ecliptic belt.

Labeling La Luna as dishonest also alludes to the tangible matter's molecular form. The physical universe is not so physical after all, as it has a temporal vibration on a subatomic level.

The creative power of visualization is in harmony with the proper seedbed of materialization. The word "magic" is contained in the spelling "I-MAGI-nation." Co-creating with the elements of nature becomes a result of imagination. The objective quest will be laced with sentimental attachment, and the hero assumes the role of a magician or a true "magi."

Star Wars: A New Hope

Meeting With the Mentor proceeds with Obi-Wan as the mentor who delivers emotionally in-depth information to the hero. Luke and Obi-Wan have a dialogue as they view R2-D2's message. This leads to Obi-Wan telling Luke about the Force and the Jedi. This wise Jedi says that the Force is omnipresent and has two sides. This represents the dual framework of electromagnetic energy. It is the substance that presides over all things.

After receiving the message from R2-D2, Obi-Wan adheres to help Princess Leia by traveling to the planet "Alderaan." The mentor pushes **The Call to Adventure** and asks the hero to join. However, Luke has yet to be invested on an emotional level, or so he thinks. Obi-Wan responds to Luke's nonacceptance and relays that one must trust their feelings.

Since the idea of the Jedi and one side of the Force was introduced, the opposing side is swiftly brought to the fore. This refers to and parallels the Moon's shadow side. Cue Pink Floyd! Two polarities are always at work and in opposition to one another in the world of duality.

In a meeting room on a battleship of the Empire, prominent generals, admirals, and the enigmatic Darth Vader gather around a large circular table. Vader argues that the Force is more potent than any Rebel Alliance threat. A generic response by overzealous Admiral Motti explains that the Force has yet to conquer the Rebels. Fearsome Darth Vader finds the admiral's scarceness of belief somewhat troubling and proves the might of the Force by telekinetically choking out Motti.

Imperial soldiers set the Skywalker ranch aflame as the narrative cuts back to Tatooine. After Luke discovers the evil side of the Moon, er, the Force, the stakes have become personal for him! The hero accepts **The Call to Adventure**, and Luke divulges to Obi-Wan he wants to become a Jedi. Let's go, young Skywalker!

Fear and Loathing in Las Vegas

Meeting With the Mentor forms in a location briefly perceived as a home. Dr. Gonzo and Hunter are safe in their hotel room as their emotional side is starting to show. Hunter receives a motherly reprimand from Gonzo for his bizarre behavior during the Gemini stage. The hero is urged to return to their fundamental essence at this moment in the adventure. A paradigm that they can use as their inner sanctuary.

Thompson's photographer for the Mint 400 event, Lacerda, enters the hotel room. He is met with a moody weariness by the heroes. Further pointing the hero in the right direction, Lacerda plays as a slight mentor and is accustomed to the Cancerian typification. He gently prods the hero to take the actions required to move forward. Lacerda displays the positive side of the Moon and shows little to no fear or hatred.

Lacerda describes the wide range of motocross bikes that will soon be present at The Mint 400. Still high on the sunshine acid, the film's point of view cuts to Hunter's perspective, and his whimsical side captures his discernment due to the Moon's misleading splendor at work. He imagines Lacerda as a military commando calling out war artillery.

During the Cancer and Capricorn seasons, there is a celebration for the Sun's vertical height above sea level at its highest peak and lowest position sanctioned by the summer and winter solstices. This hero's journey celebration is represented as The Mint 400 and highlights the summer solstice.

When the film shifts to the motocross event, Hunter Thompson goes through it with thrill and excitement. However, soon after, the motorcyclists coagulate a dust cloud, and the Moon's deceiving effects render the sense of sight null and void. The latter degrees of this step on the astrological wheel resembles a passing psychological state that can manifest as potentially choppy waters.

The film cuts to Hunter and Lacerda navigating the dust storm in a Humvee. Lacerda says they must obtain full reportage since the situation makes him exceedingly blissful. Hunter gets out of the Humvee physically and emotionally exhausted by the circumstances. As Thompson exits the vehicle, a shot shows Lacerda's reaction, and the Moon is appropriately displayed in the distance. As Lacerda drives away, Hunter is left alone in the desert and in a sea of susceptibilities.

Superbad

The stakes have increased for **Meeting With the Mentor** as the first water sign begins at Evan's residence after school. Seth reserves a metaphorical shell on his back and upholds an inner sense of home comparable to the crab of Cancer that carries its shell where it goes. He chisels his quintessential essence into anything by using a wardrobe change.

This switch of outfits illustrates the primary function of a mentor figure. The hero is given a supernatural gift, demonstrated by Seth dressing in Evan's dad's clothing. He is fostering a sense of safety and comfort that functions as a shield to prepare the hero for entering the **Special World**.

In the following scene, McLovin meets Seth and Evan in front of a supermarket liquor store. Seth declares that McLovin's fake ID was an idiotic idea. He is basing his claim on the Moon's fraudulent sensitivities, the solar archetype plans to collect all the alcohol and pick up the Moon's components one at a time.

Movie magic ensues inside the supermarket liquor store as the film shows Seth's imagination conjuring various scenarios. One scene depicts him helping an older woman who fits the mold of a maternal figure connected to the subject of comfort explored in Cancer. Seth assists this older woman with her shopping procurement, and she quickly purchases all the alcohol he requires. However, the hero's imagination fails to persist and slowly fades away. Seth abandons his scheme empty-handed. The hero's visualization subdues his tenacity.

Trainspotting

The boys enter the club and initiate the fourth stage, **Meeting With the Mentor**. Renton makes a reference in narration to acting on instinct rather than reason. He describes how the need for sexual relations has become his primary attraction.

The Cancer exemplar and the mentor figure Diane is made visible in a crowded club by a bright light on her glittering Moon-like dress. She plays as a mentor who will help guide and further lead the hero forward. Renton pursues her and narrates his enchantment. Diane prepares to exit the club, and Renton does so shortly after.

Diane (the Moon) and Renton (the Sun) converge outside and have a dialogue scene. She is initially apathetic but accepting of his bold nature. When Renton inquires about her destination, she responds that she is heading to her abode. To elicit deeper feelings, Diane starts to pierce Renton's way of living verbally by probing into his basic philosophy of life. This mentor is striving to make the hero's feelings more prominent.

Diane then enters the backseat of a taxi, and Renton is subtly invited to join. Later that night, when they sleep together at Diane's house, our hero's perspective is engulfed by the glistening seas and moonlit waters. The following morning, Diane's parents are seated in the kitchen. Renton casually pulls up a chair as if these were his parents and exemplify the coziness of home. When Diane enters the scene wearing her high school uniform, Mark Renton is confident that the emotional stakes have risen.

Mean Girls

A Halloween party replicating the summer solstice celebration initiates **Metting With the Mentor**. Cady portrays the persona of the lunar wanderer while wearing a silvery gown of a bride zombie. Regina dresses as a scantily clad bunny and represents the solar energy of Aries. Rabbits are an animal totem that embodies the innocence of the rising Aries Sun, which has a spring in its step resembling the Nothern Hemisphere's springtime.

On a side note, the rabbit is the first character Alice encounters in *Alice in Wonderland*. After spotting him, Alice chases the white rabbit and enters the rabbit hole. And thus, her amazing trip starts. The movie *The Matrix* and Jefferson Airplane's 1967 song, "*White Rabbit*," which some claim was about ingesting LSD, both use the white rabbit to symbolize setting out on a quest. The hare thus stands for Aries and the beginning of an escapade.

Back to *Mean Girls*, Regina illustrates the kaleidoscopic side of the Moon's elusive character and plants a seed of untruth in Aaron's head regarding Cady. In front of Cady, Regina kisses Aaron. This moment tugs at the hero's emotional heartstrings. This drives **The Call to Adventure** into irreversible emotional arousal.

Cady leaves the party severely upset and is welcomed by Janis and Damian with open arms. Janis plays the mentor role, laying down a well-thought-out game plan to advance the protagonist into the **Special World**. Cady can follow this route to shoehorn the desolation of Regina and the Plastics. The hero announces that she accepts the mission since the stakes have become personal.

The antics continue as the film cuts to the Plastics' methodical downfall in montage fashion. Cady comments on the need for covert maneuvering to complete this task. In a dialogue sequence between Regina and Cady, it is revealed that Janis is allegedly a lesbian. The flavor of close relationships and the flexibility of movements within the ideology or orientation is suggested.

Damian distributes Secret Santa gifts as the fourth stage concludes. He is dressed as Santa Claus, mimicking Cancer's opposite season in

Capricorn. As Glen Coco receives four candy canes from Damian, an oblique reference to the fourth sign of the zodiac is made.

Snatch

Gorgeous George and Tommy pull into the Irish gypsy campground to buy a new caravan as they embark on **Meeting With the Mentor**. Gorgeous George brandishes the psychic propensity of the water element and foretells how this situation will get chaotic.

The Cancer and Capricorn axis symbolizes the inner and outer world and displays an actual exterior and interior dominion. The caravans in this film represent an external and internal kingdom called home. Gypsies or "pikeys" continually shift geographically like the Moon's various lunar phases. The pikeys convey this idea of home while maintaining their traditional way of life.

The Irish pikey Mickey O'Neil is featured in this stage as a Cancer archetype and embodies the solstice. As the focal point of the interrelated events, Mickey is somewhat of the movie's "soul." He also pushes Turkish and Tommy to progress on their journey as the mentor archetype who provokes the film's myriad events. Mickey resembles the Sun in Cancer in that he possesses supreme physical prowess and takes the role of a likable character.

Mickey formally introduces himself and his mum to Tommy and Gorgeous George. Mum O'Neil is an example of the maternal archetype. As stray dogs are all over the gypsy camp, Mrs. O'Neil offers Tommy a drink and asks him if he fancies dogs. With the arrival of settlers, dogs are said to be companion species for individuals destined to travel. As colonial animals, dogs are intertwined with citizenship, cultural affiliation, and settling down. As a generic metaphor for "man's best friend" and the physical representation of consciousness and conscious awareness, dogs are used to symbolize both. Let me explain.

Because it is a physiological aspect of human consciousness emerging in concrete reality, witnessing an animal is a sign from the spiritual realm. Animals are distinctive animated physical representations of specific emotions and energetic fragments of awareness. Dogs can bare a connection to the physical manifestations of attention reflected in the human mind, making them natural companions of humans.

Souls, limitless beings, are put inside a human body to study and develop while exercising control. Animals were revered as spirit guides in ancient Egypt. Because animals are a real-time reflection of one's consciousness from the spirit realm, the Egyptians revered them as gods and treated them as royalty.

The word "canine" has a similar sound to the word "Cancer." The constellations Canis Major, Canis Minor, and the Dog-Star Sirius are all near the sign of Cancer along the ecliptic belt. According to the ancient Egyptians, Sirius has been associated with the astrological attributes of the fourth sign since the beginning of human history. Sirius is also linked to a facet of the goddess Isis of the ancient culture. Sirius outlines the likeness of the absolute divine feminine in the zodiac's first water sign. This point in the astrological year energizes the summer season. In this way, the divine feminine serves as both a gateway and frequently as the force that gives life to our desires.

Back to *Snatch*, misleading glamour is demonstrated as Tommy and Gorgeous George prepare to exit the campsite in their freshly purchased caravan, but it breaks down before they can leave. Mickey offers to challenge Gorgeous George to a dual over the dispute. It is revealed during the fight that Mickey honors the source of the energy that flows through him by kissing his necklace before he swings. He KO's Gorgeous George with one punch as if he has the Midas Touch. The song *"Golden Brown"* is playing, and Tommy better hope Gorgeous George gets up, or else he'll be inconspicuously interred with him.

5

LEO - CROSSING THE FIRST THRESHOLD

This phase follows the highest peak and the initial ascent after the roller coaster's severe plunge. For the final stage of the first act, the characters let loose and are called forth to embody the means of learning how to express their individual star quality while **Crossing the First Threshold**. The soul essence imprinted by the flame of the highest source is singular and unique.

Leo is summoning a concentrated glow and urging the hero to maintain passion fiercely. The feline is the gatekeeper at the entryway. The heroes must embody the lion and pass through the gateway into the **Special World** of the cinematic environment.

How will the hero express their obligation to fulfill their desire now that they know what they want and who they are? What style of song will they sing? How might their wish be inventively satiated? Loud and proud now! This stage develops one's capacity to trust their instincts by promoting a spirit for self-dignity.

The Sun is at its highest point in the Nothern Hemisphere in Cancer, while it is at its warmest in Leo. The Sun is linked to the electrical awareness of the ego and masculine power. The "I," or the ego, serves as our point of contact with the outside world and should be enjoyed by everyone. The ego so carefully preserved up to this point in the journey is prepared to have a moment of pure exuberance since it has learned the required lessons. The hero is becoming bolder with each step.

The five-pointed star resembles the human form and corresponds to the zodiac's fifth sign. This significant number establishes a link to the elements — fire, earth, air, and water — that have all been encountered on the journey thus far. In this second fire sign, the sparkle of spirit imprints a one-of-a-kind soul signature to assert the four elements with source energy while also experiencing the fifth element, Ether, also known as "Aether" in Greek. Ether is the definition of atmospheric essence.

By summoning a divine connection and collaborating with warmheartedness to manifest, the hero is taking on the attributes of the Sun. The show's star, the light of day, through photosynthesis, improves the human body by energizing vivacity and electrically charged motivation.

Star Wars: A New Hope

Luke engages in **Crossing the First Threshold** and enters the spaceport "Moss Eisley." This is a location that highlights the wide variety of characters that exist in the **Special World**.

The band plays a tune as Obi-Wan and Luke walk into the cosmic saloon full of different alien species. The idea of entertainment is expressed in the fun and games section of the journey and corresponds to the avant-garde sign of Leo.

Luke attracts an unwanted bystander's attention, which causes the focus of the entire cantina to shift to a specific region of the establishment, similar to how the Sun can only highlight particular areas of the Earth's surface. Obi-Wan displays the Force's might and charm as he uses his saber of light to chop off the arm of the threat. This demonstrates Leo's daring electric nature. The danger is eliminated, and the music resumes as the cantina returns to normalcy.

Han Solo, a space smuggler, and his companion Chewbacca, a furry "Wookie," are introduced as Leo embodiments. Han Solo has a certain level of male masculinity that aligns with the electrical Yang paradigm of this fixed fire sign. At the same time, Chewbacca displays a literal feline demeanor and a temperament to match. Han agrees to accept payment in exchange for flying Obi-Wan and Luke to Alderaan aboard his vintage ship, "The Millennium Falcon."

In the following scene, the bounty hunter Greedo enters the bar to collect a bounty on the head of Han Solo. This moment puts Han's machismo to the test. Solo's wit and charm save him from the awkward situation as he shoots first! Greedo is stopped, and another spotlight is shone on a specific area in the saloon.

Fear and Loathing in Las Vegas

As they embark on **Crossing the First Threshold**, Hunter and Gonzo put the true American dream into motion. Bring on the Tom Jones tunes! On the Vegas strip, the heroes incite revelry.

In narration, Thompson describes Las Vegas as a location fit for wealthy people of high status. While stepping fully into exuding charisma, the hero is considering adopting a royal manner.

Hunter and Gonzo wander to the entrance of the Debbie Reynolds concert venue. Large gold-plated doors leading to an entry are attractively displayed, glittering like the rays of the Sun as though the doors were the gates the heroes had to cross to reach the first initiation. They are immediately rejected once they enter, as they hysterically laugh uncontrollably.

The film segways to our solar deities ingesting the drug "Ether," comparable to the fifth element and the fifth stage. The fifth element, which symbolizes the fuller manifestation of a higher spirit beyond the human form, moves one from physicality into energies that cannot be seen.

The heroes enter the "Bazooka Circus" extremely intoxicated. Advertisements for excess and extravagant feelings are presented throughout the circus to highlight the Sun in Leo. The sensory overload of the Bazooka Circus is exhibited as the blazing daylight scolds too hot.

Dr. Gonzo and Hunter seek refuge in a rotating carousel bar. The heroes look like two lions in a circus ring sitting on a rotating bar. A lion statue on the carousel's edge is woven into the borders of the set decoration. This well-known ride can be seen as a symbolic imitation of the Sun's year-round, constant motion through the astrological signs.

Dr. Gonzo's inability to walk straight causes the fun and games segment to lean towards hedonism. He wants to leave the slowly rotating carousel bar but cannot do so as the waitress kicks him out because of his brass behavior. During the latter part of the Leo section, the heroes can develop immoderate self-indulgence.

Superbad

Bringing about the Leo segment and wrapping up the first act, McLovin is instructed by Seth and Evan on what to redeem for Jule's party in the parking lot of another liquor store. Will McLovin have the lion's courage? Not yet, as he hesitates, **Crossing the First Threshold**.

Seth threatens McLovin by telling him that if he does not enter, he will tear this face off and wear it as a mask. An act that a wild animal might do. McLovin eventually musters up the courage to cross the threshold's gates.

Seth and Evan stand back when they notice a familiar face strolling her dog down the street. They reveal their infatuation and rush over for a better look. The two resemble lions stalking their prey.

Returning to McLovin's breach of the threshold, he is greeted by Mindy, who works behind the counter. She represents a Leo archetype and a guardian the hero must meet before crossing the entryway. She is garbed in a red shirt adhering to the element of fire. McLovin's identification passes the test, but a criminal robbing the liquor store knocks McLovin from his high perch.

Seth and Evan notice a police cruiser outside the liquor store when they emerge from their stalk. They now must act courageously in their own right. Officer Michaels and Officer Slater, two new Leo archetypes, are introduced inside the store. The two cops exhibit self-respecting traits and serve as another boundary protector. The police accept Mclovin's ID and question him, but they do so in good humor. They kindly offer McLovin a ride into the **Special World** since he earned his stripes.

Trainspotting

The four leads pause from the usual routine to start the Leo portion and the second fire sign. They depart on a train and navigate the first threshold into the Scottish countryside. One of the earliest alchemical symbols is the green lion devouring the Sun, which draws a connection to the sign of Leo and the green heart chakra. Since the Sun is the source of photosynthesis, green is the most noticeable color in this scene.

Tommy directs the course while the boys are in the green pastures since his joyful demeanor fits well with the Sun's home sign. Tommy expresses his belief in loving oneself. He advises his pals to take pride in being Scottish.

Renton exclaims with arrogance that being Scottish is pure rubbish! He is unwilling to accept his ancestry in a tenderhearted manner. Renton indicates burning the wick at both ends in the final part of this fiery stage.

Mean Girls

The Leo segment opens with a holiday talent event, and the characters are prepared to woo **Crossing the First Threshold** with a charismatically engaging attitude. The plastics perform a choreographed dance they perform every year that mirrors the Sun's continual yearly journey.

Moments before the curtain rises, Regina gives Gretchen the order to switch to her other side. As Capricorn is dominated by the formidable taskmaster Saturn, Gretchen, seen as the Capricorn prototype, falls to last place throughout the Leo season.

The plastics perform their routine but are forced to change course when Gretchen accidentally bumps into the stereo and knocks it off the stage. The remainder of the song is then sung in unison by everyone in the audience. This instance showcases the school's artistic abilities in the expressively stimulating sign.

The Leo stage continues as Gretchen loses her cool when presenting a paper on Julius Caesar in class. She inadvertently draws comparisons between Regina and Julius Caesar's overt authoritarian use of leadership. The lion, who rules the jungle, is regarded as domineering in its ability to exert strong willpower.

In narration, Cady compares the Plastic lifestyle to being in the limelight. She undoubtedly appreciates the attention of the public. The first act concludes with a montage featuring a variety of personalities responding to the gossip about the Plastics — cue the Missy Elliot music!

Snatch

Vinny and Solomon, two new characters, are introduced during the Leo segment of the wheel. Vinny and Sol stand for "The Lions of the Tribe of Judah" and Leo personifications. One of Israel's twelve tribes, the Tribe of Judah, is most associated with the lion. The name "Solomon" is connected to the phrase "Soul of Man" and includes the phrases "Sol and Mon," which are synonymous with Sun and Moon.

Vinny walks inside Solomon's pawnshop, and shortly after that, Boris The Blade shows up. Boris offers the Leo archetypes $50,000 to rob the bookmakers of Brick Top's illegal boxing bout. They heed the summons and successfully agree to cross the first cinematic passageway. This event sparks a series of events that will affect the entire ensemble of characters.

In the following scene, the getaway driver Tyrone, who portrays another Leo expression, is also introduced. His pleasingly round body exudes confidence in his mobility, similar to the Sun chugging along without fail.

Turkish and Tommy are without a boxer after Mickey injured Gorgeous George, and they're suddenly in Brick Top's debt. Turkish concludes after the film continues through **Crossing the First**

Threshold that Mickey will be the fighter in Brick Top's forthcoming fixed match.

6

VIRGO - TESTS, ALLIES, ENEMIES

At the beginning of the second act, the heroes realize they must turn their energetic emotions into something worthwhile. Words become flesh after passing through the heart of the lion and into the mutable earth sign of Virgo.

At this sixth stage, the imagination and fiery vigor of the hero are disciplined. The emphasis in **Tests, Allies, Enemies** is honing and molding the glimmer of bravery into something materially tangible.

Mercury, the celestial nomad who rules Virgo, brings forth a mental refinement in which one distinguishes and categorizes what is beneficial and frees oneself from potential restraints. The hero must choose what else to perfect before becoming great masters of their trade. What Jedi abilities do you hold, Neo?

This mutable earth sign is analytical and compels pertinent data for impeding situations. As the sign that rules the digestive system, separating the wheat from the chaff, Virgo governs the harvest before autumn in the Northern Hemisphere while consuming the food from the Sun.

The virgin, an interpretive depiction of purity, appears as the symbol for the sixth zodiac sign; Virgo themes appear to carry out a duty perfectly harmoniously with the divine. The idea of perfection is needed before the essential descent into the opposing signs. Indicating a state of purification to prepare the hero for imperilment up ahead.

Joseph Campbell has a category dubbed "**Meeting with the Goddess**" at this stage in *The Hero With A Thousand Faces*. The revelation of the magnificence of the hero's counterpart provides a glimmer of holiness for the remainder of the voyage.

Star Wars: A New Hope

The Greek myth Hades and Persephone takes shape and allegorically symbolizes the sign of Virgo. The goddess Persephone (the Sun in Virgo) is captured by Hades and taken to the underworld, where she is kept there for six months.

In the myth, a deal is agreed upon that Persephone will spend six months of the year in the underworld and can only return to the surface for the other six months. The Sun will soon "fall" into the following six nocturnal zodiac signs, leaving behind its dominant position in the sky and entering the "underworld."

Princess Leia is on board the war station of the Empire, the "Death Star." Hades, I mean Darth Vader, commands Leia to reveal the whereabouts of R2-D2, who has the technical readouts of the Death Star, or risk having Leia's home planet, Alderaan, destroyed. Leia can disclose the droids' location or watch her home be demolished. She eventually caves, but Darth Vader, a.k.a Hades, proceeds with his scheme and blows the planet Alderaan sky-high.

The heroes manage to exit Moss Eisley in the Millennium Falcon and jump to hyper-speed. Luke has assembled his allies and will now learn to perfect his abilities as a Jedi while preparing for the next attack from the adversary.

Obi-Wan lends a hand in guiding Luke in the infancy of his Jedi training. Giving shape to the magnetic subconscious essence of Virgo, the wise Jedi tells the young student to let go of his conscious self and learn to trust his intuition.

Fear and Loathing in Las Vegas

Hunter and Dr. Gonzo return to their hotel room while buzzing from the Leo festivities. Virgo oversees the harvest of fruits and vegetables, which brings to pass a discussion about limes and how none grow in the desert. Gonzo starts to slice the limes and maintains a furious composition.

In a flashback scene, a television reporter acted by Virgo Sun sign Cameron Diaz is seen with the photographer Lacerda in a crowded elevator. Hunter and Gonzo swiftly enter. She embodies a goddess and Virgo archetype and exudes respect for Dr. Gonzo. The reporter mistakenly and respectfully remarks Gonzo must be one of the motocross riders, seeing a more refined version.

Dr. Gonzo participates in the act while feigning more notoriety. He appears pretty tidy and is wearing a salmon-colored shirt. This pertains to the cleanliness associated with the Virgo philosophy of keeping everything organized and spotless. Another person in the elevator calls out Dr. Gonzo while he is engaged in flirtatious behavior with the television reporter. Gonzo makes a hasty judgment and openly lashes out at Lacerda. In the last degrees of mercurial Virgo, when thoughts are manifested through deeds, this can encourage the capacity to become outwardly paranoid.

As the film returns to the present moment, Thompson observes Gonzo's state of mind. Thompson exits the hotel room slowly and cautiously as he presents a state of slight paranoia.

Superbad

Seth and Evan are still in the liquor store parking lot for the start of the second act and the Virgo stage. Seth yells neurotically that they need to take action immediately as they argue about their next step. They are reminded of physicality when Francis, a new character, is introduced and accidentally backs his car into Seth. Francis is a persona that represents a nervous, agitated Virgo mentality. He apologizes for backing into Seth and offers an invitation to another party. Seth seizes this chance now that McLovin is gone. Before continuing with the rest of the astrological adventure, the hero must gather some form of a harvest.

The main characters are seen riding around in Francis' car, and Mercury, the ruler of Virgo, reveals the use of a communication tool. Seth receives a call from a goddess embodied by Jules. Seth assures her he is still on his way by expressing the Sun's yearly continuous passage despite all delays.

Cut to McLovin riding in the squad car and being escorted to the party by the two cops. They talk about how Officer Michaels is a rookie cop who has only been on the job for six months, giving a nod to the sixth sign of the zodiac. Maintaining a commitment to developing one's skills and personal craft, Officer Slater mentions Jedi techniques and references *Star Wars*. He compares Office Michaels to a newly trained "Padawan." An incident at a local bar is suddenly reported to the cops. The Sun insists on descending into the depths every year without fail, so they tell McLovin they must accept.

Trainspotting

A course of action is adhered to before the Sun's upcoming annual slope; thus, Renton resumes using the scag. During a dialogue scene, Sick Boy and Renton compare heroin to "Bond Girls." Virgo's magnetic traits in action can equate to a super soldier or secret agent, a refined form of feminine magnetic attraction.

Trainspotting's overtly gritty undertone emphasizes the excess of focusing on one's desires and needs while ignoring the finer details of life as the crew continues their presumptuous ways.

Mean Girls

After romping through Leo's explosive masculine sign, the hero melts into a magnetic complexion in Virgo. This level represents the intersection of the divine masculine and feminine forces as a harmonious union.

The **Tests, Allies, Enemies** stage begins as Cady and Aaron Samuels jointly learn math at Cady's house while participating in proficient knowledge. Education is a proponent of Virgo and shows the concept of studying and gaining wisdom. Proper education is extracting one's skill set instead of general systematic indoctrination.

As a result of their discourse, they kiss and establish a sacred bond. After Virgo's holiness is found, Aaron withdraws in response. Cady reveals Regina's infidelity by providing pertinent statistics.

The setting for the next scene is Regina's house, where Cady and Karen join her. Regina's reaction to learning that Aaron had broken up with her is shown, and we eventually see how devastated Regina is as she exits the scene in an uproar.

A conversation between Cady and Karen comes to pass, and Cady draws attention to Karen's talents as an example of how the Sun is developing her feminine aptness. Cady maintains that Karen must retain some capabilities.

Karen admits she has "ESP," and she can tell when it will rain, making a connection to her embodiment of the psyche-based fourth sign of the zodiac. This instance also exemplifies harmony with the natural cycles.

As the journey progresses, Cady finalizes her transformation into a pristine Plastic. She is a candidate for "The Spring Fling" queen. Fine-tuned to her job and immersed in her temperament, she expresses her mercurial thoughts in The Burn Book. Cady writes about how she believes Ms. Norbury is a drug dealer while acting like the ideal Plastic.

The hero completes her transformation and is on the peak of the forthcoming descent into the quest's second half. She informs Janis and Damian that she has developed well-thought-out plans to carry out her evil, crafty schemes.

Snatch

Doug The Head and Avi have a phone conversation in which they further discuss a strategy for locating Franky Four Fingers and the diamond. After the deliberation, Avi boards a flight to London in a montage sequence. Given that Virgo is a mutable earth sign, the airplane montage depicts Virgo's connection to a changing world and the transmutation of movable soil.

Starting the heist to rob the bookies, Sol and Vinny sit in their car and decide to proceed. During the robbery, a woman behind the counter tells them the bets are off. She embodies a Virgo ideal and dishes out the unreserved truth of the situation.

Unsuccessfully robbing the bookies, Sol and Vinny at least manage to get their hands on the diamond. However, there is a catch: the suitcase is tied to Franky's arm. The Leo's capture the Aries archetype during the Virgo phase to soon hand over the Sun (the diamond) to the Libra exemplar.

Tommy and Turkish accept Mickey's offer to fight. They agree to buy a caravan for his Ma. If all goes according to plan, a new caravan for the nomad should be doable in exchange for staying alive. The film cuts to Brick Top's rigged match. Mickey is to throw the fight in the fourth round, but he knocks out his opponent in the first few seconds. Brick Top loses and admits that putting his trust in the pikey was a mistake while discovering the importance of having faith in his discernment.

7

—•—

LIBRA - APPROACH TO THE INMOST CAVE

A reciprocation of shared sunlight performs a balancing act of opposites and ironically presents the idea that change is the only constant.

The heroes have reasoned how to reduce flawlessness to perfection. Whether asking questions or playing with an option, the hero will start to wonder who is involved and what significant decisions they must make as they enter the **Approach to the Inmost Cave**.

From Virgo's grounded, detail-oriented aspects, the quest transitions into the seventh stage of Libra and the beginning of the nocturnal signs of the astrological wheel. The journey's first half is spent developing a healthy ego, and the second half is spent turning inside and letting go of the ego construct.

Darkness reigns when the Sun goes down, but there is immense beauty in a sunset and the understanding that the sunlight must be divvied up. The assimilation of the fundamental prerequisite for paradoxical contradictions is established. The accomplishment of the first half reinforces the desire for closure, increasing our capacity to comprehend how the self develops through relationships.

Willing to kick start stimulus as all the cardinal signs do, in Libra, stimulation is started by relating to the outside world via a viewpoint and a counter viewpoint. The hero in Libra becomes aware of how life is played. This game of Yin and Yang explores the concept of coexistence — the other aids in our understanding of the self.

Libra is a warrior sign since the cardinal air element imparts justice and fairness for all. Speaking and interacting are two ways the essence of air calls consciousness out to perform. The hero takes on an outward action trajectory since Libra is a powerful, electrical sign.

Star Wars: A New Hope

The Empire exhibits the power shift, and the heroes emerge from hyperspace and land into the scattered fragments of wrecked Alderaan drifting into space. The antagonistic pull from the opposite side causes the outer objective to switch to a new purpose and the heroes are drawn inside the Death Star. Following rather than leading takes shape.

Two imperial troopers wait outside the Falcon as two more troopers board with scanners. The heroes devise a group strategy and switch clothes while the good guys pose as the bad guys. Han and Luke portray paradoxical versions of themselves covered in the enemy's armor. A course of action in Libra is created by building a perspective shift that encourages increasing cohesiveness.

Unnoticed, the heroes enter the control room, R2-D2 connects to the Imperial network, and a new mission is launched. R2 locates the tractor beam's power source, and the heroes learn that Princess Leia will be executed. The task now resolves around getting away.

A balancing act of alternatives is offered as Han and Luke disagree over the best action. Luke adopts a different strategy for advancing than straightforward action. He becomes convincing and persuades Han to save the Princess since she will generously reward him for doing so by appealing to the ideology of the other. A balanced win-win situation. While the others try to save the Princess, Obi-Wan plans to turn off the source of the tractor beam.

Fear and Loathing in Las Vegas

At the start of Libra, Thompson departs the hotel suite to let Gonzo ferment alone. At 4 am, he strolls into the casino; a wind-related sound in the background plays and refers to the air element. Hunter's analysis in narration puts the isolated feeling amid the crowded casino in its proper perspective. The hero enters the **Approach to the Inmost Cave** while remarking on his seclusiveness.

Hunter observes the other gamblers in the casino and narrates how this is a terrible parody of the American ideal. His voice-over describes how, while surrounded by people, he ironically cannot connect.

The protagonist in this stage is figuratively or literally laying down bets for future results and demonstrating how gambling coincides with the seventh sign. Hunter engages in a game of roulette to potentially profit from various options.

Superbad

Cardinal air intervenes to improve people's lives in a social context; the cops and McLovin access the **Approach to the Inmost Cave** at a nearby bar. The cops try to control the situation, but the offender escapes. McLovin unintentionally causes the perpetrator to stumble before taking off. He lays down the gavel of justice. An impartial, unbiased verdict is made directly to something becoming collectively fair.

Cut to Francis guiding Evan and Seth towards the entrance of the deepest cave, which he refers to as a dome of thunder. This can relate to the electrical, masculine mode of Libra. Evan and Seth can engage with the larger community at this house party, a prime representation of interrelations. They had previously avoided situations like this, but now they take decisive action and dovetail into them; the heroes must deal with many individuals of all shapes and sizes.

Upon entry, Francis is about to make a phone call demonstrating the connection between air and interpersonal communication. Francis is forcibly dragged out of the house in disapproval and with a swift judgment by Mark, the homeowner, and a Libra persona. Seth and Evan must depart immediately or remain and suffer the same outcome. As Seth stays and Evan leaves, the scales create a delicate balance.

Trainspotting

In *Trainspotting*, the midpoint is introduced with the same shot as the movie's beginning, in which the protagonists flee from the police at high speed. Renton can no longer do his business in the same manner. The Gemini archetype Sick Boy manages to escape, but Renton and Spud are caught.

The scene shifts to a courthouse with judges presiding over the diplomatic sign. As a result of his participation in a rehabilitation program, Renton receives a light penalty, tipping the scales of justice in his favor.

The film then cuts to the ensemble cast enjoying a pint at a local pub. There is a sense of communal living as all the characters converse in one location. However, Renton describes his need for more profound sensations, which pushes him into the upcoming stage of Scorpio.

Mean Girls

The Plastics are having a group conversation broadcast over the Libra airwaves on a 4-way phone call. The throne is formally transferred to the Libra portion of the cross the following day at school when Regina is expelled from the Plastics hierarchy. Gretchen and Karen follow Cady everywhere, demonstrating the hero's ability to manipulate others around her, as she claims in narration.

After her parents have left for the evening, Cady throws a house party to welcome in the **Approach to the Inmost Cave**. This party causes several personalities to merge, and Cady starts exploring the issues from the opposite direction. She plans to avoid inviting her adversarial archetype to fully cultivate her successful promotion.

Although ramming to her disadvantage, Regina shows up at the party and verbalizes the audacity of Cady not inviting her. The Sun in Aries rightfully blazed the trail for the other zodiac signs.

Aaron eventually shows up at the gathering and admits his infatuation for Cady. They have another private consolidation while alone in Cady's bedroom. However, things start to go south during their talk. Cady painstakingly expresses her words more in line with how the Plastics communicate, and the drinks begin to speak for her. The final degrees of Libra can bring up conversations that are piercingly razor-sharp. As a result, Cady begins to word vomit before actually doing so onto her golden calf Aaron Samuels.

Snatch

Referring to two members of the gods of ancient Egypt, Osiris governed Egypt peacefully. Still, his envious brother Set wanted the throne and slayed him. He minced Osiris's body, distributed the pieces across the land, and claimed the throne. Set represents the Sun as it is setting and corresponds to the Sun moving into the sign of Libra.

Aries specimen Franky Four Fingers or Osiris is defeated by Boris The Blade, the Libra embodiment or Set. The Sun now resides in the sign of Libra after Boris removes the suitcase containing the diamond.

Brick Top portrays the great taskmaster Saturn and the opposing side as he is fully empowered at this time. When Turkish returns to his arcade company, he sees Brick Top waiting. Brick Top takes Turkish's life savings from his safe and demands to use Mickey for his forthcoming rigged fight. The film follows Brick Top as he leaves the arcade and tells his thugs to find the bookies' robbers.

Tommy and Turkish go to Mickey's campsite, where he is "hare coursing." When Turkish and Tommy encourage him to participate in the fight, Mickey responds that he will only do it if they purchase him an even bigger caravan than the first. The heroes place a wager regarding the dispute on a rabbit traversing an open field with two hounds hunting it in light of the themes of Libra pertaining to placing bets.

Tommy and Turkish wager on the hounds, while Mickey bets on the hare. This sequence in the film alludes to a star-based storyline and symbolically represents the Sun entering Libra. This montage offers levels of esoteric depth.

Near the beginning of the zodiac on the ecliptic belt, the constellation Lepus, which means "hare" in Latin, is found beneath the Orion constellation. As described in prior chapters, the animal symbol for Aries, the sign that opposes Libra, is a rabbit or hare due to the Aries Sun being related to the idea of starting "pure" and embarking on a new beginning.

Near Lepus the hare, is the "big dog" and "the little dog" constellations called Canis Major and Canis Minor. Sirius, the brightest
star, also called "the Dog-Star," is inside Canis Major. Orion's hunting
hounds chasing the hare in the starry sky are likened to Canis Major
and Canis Minor. It is possible to interpret this scene from *Snatch* as
a direct allusion to these constellations.

From a comparative standpoint, the two dogs in this sequence are
Canis Major and Canis Minor, and the hare symbolizes the Sun in
Aries and the constellation Lepus. The Sun or the hare are potentially
being devoured by the two dogs, which would cause the Sun to "fall"
into Libra.

Despite the Sun's annual descent to the lower reaches of the sky, it
consistently manages to regain its previous position; this is shown by
the hare escaping the hunt. This is an allegory for how the Sun always
rises and sets despite the Sun's annual descent further away from the
equator on the ecliptic belt's latter half.

When the cosmic sub-story involving the stars is over, Mickey wins
the bet, and Turkish and Tommy are required to buy a new caravan.
The hero's goal, in the beginning, was to buy a caravan for themselves,
but by the end of Libra, the plan completely shifts; the heroes must
now purchase a caravan for another.

8

SCORPIO - THE ORDEAL

What is the impact of the verdict that the heroes have confirmed and weighed in the previous proceedings? In Libra, the protagonists have learned the art of making essential decisions while considering the perspectives of others; in Scorpio, there is no longer a choice.

Fun and games marked the beginning of the transfer into the **Special Word** in the sign of Leo, which leads to things becoming translucently real in **The Ordeal**. The hero will suffer an emptiness during this eighth stage and give birth to a phoenix emerging from the fragmented wreckage. This is the "mini climax" of the second act. There is an internal struggle taking place within the protagonist's awareness.

Value was placed upon the physical self in Taurus, Scorpio's opposite sign, but now the focus is on the shadow side. As something transmutes into the stratosphere, importance is placed on the mysterious aspect of life. The hero is presented with a gift after facing the truth of the shadow self. Genuineness is viewed as the greatest treasure rather than a barrier.

Joseph Campbell refers to this gift of truth as the "**Ultimate Boon**." Moral principles are updated while the hero is freed from a victim mentality. They look into what is hidden in the most remote dark places, gaining an improved new viewpoint and recognizing inspirational empowerment. The heroes transform into an assimilation of everything they have fully committed to.

Star Wars: A New Hope

Luke and Han enter the detention facility dressed as Storm Troopers and immediately conduct **The Ordeal**. Chewbacca poses as a prisoner who escapes, and Luke and Han use their weapons to break through the line of defense. After removing all the guards, our heroes almost escape while rescuing Leia.

Darth Vader is shown in the following scene sensing the change in the Force. The Force is boiling to the surface in Scorpio's receptive and magnetic vibrations. When the commander of the Death Star, Grand Moff Tarkin, informs Vader that the Jedi have been wiped out for years, the cell bay activates an emergency alert. Vader affirms Scorpio's capacity to face the danger head-on and asserts that he must confront the reality of the situation.

The shadow and terror take center stage, with Storm Troopers encircling any exit from the cell bay. The heroes' whereabouts are known throughout the system, according to C3-PO, who distributes the information to Luke via a transmitter. The group successfully exits the bay and enters the "belly of the whale."

A magnetically enclosed sewage compactor serves as a visual representation of this hidden psychological experience. Luke (the Sun) is drawn into the watery depths of Scorpio by a living sewer creature. Hope is slowly eroding as the walls close in around them.

Adhering to a three-act structure, each zodiac sign contains three separate phases. The sign of Scorpio can be assigned to three animals:

a scorpion, a hawk, and a phoenix. The scorpion gives form to the frightening side of this sign, the hawk shows the capacity to gain a broader perspective after the terrifying phase is finished, and the phoenix symbolizes the fiery bird rising from the trial of evolutionary transmutation.

When C3-PO and R2-D2 stop all electrical systems, the third phase of Scorpio, represented by a phoenix, steps in to save the day. As Obi-Wan turns off the tractor beam, Luke and the others escape the waste compactor. The heroes reappear after **The Ordeal**, stronger and more alive than before.

Fear and Loathing in Las Vegas

Thompson is called into a sticky scenario for the eighth stage in the hotel suite bathroom. Dr. Gonzo puts on display **The Ordeal** while submerged in the watery depths of "Davey Jone's Locker" as he is exhaustively strung out in the murky bathwater. Gonzo pulls out his large dagger that resembles the stinger of a scorpion's tail and points it at Hunter.

Jefferson Airplane's "*White Rabbit*" plays on a tape player, and Gonzo orders Hunter to throw it into the bathtub to convey a sense of detachment when *White Rabbit* peaks. The hero grants his request by throwing a heavy fruit in his direction instead. As soon as he leaves, Hunter locks the door behind him.

The solar hero finds sanctuary on the couch after calming the uncomfortable situation. The film enters the depths of the hero's subjective state in a flashback scene at a psychedelic club called "The Matrix."

During the flashback, the hero notices an older version of himself, played by the real Hunter S. Thompson, casually seated in the crowded radical club. By physically viewing himself from an unbiased perspective, Thompson gazes into the waters of his authentic self.

The movie continues the flashback with Hunter using a narcotic in the bathroom of The Matrix. A second hippie enters the bathroom and joins in on the partaking of the drug. The Scorpio stage reaches its peak when a conventional business person walks in and sees the hippies openly consuming the mind-altering drug. This scenario shows how certain moments can alter one's established point of view.

Superbad

Watching the security tape of McLovin from the liquor store, the cops and McLovin relax with a few celebratory brews. McLovin is learning to "take a hit," and the opportunity to view one's situation objectively from a higher vantage point is presented.

When the conversation turns to sexual content, the officers assert that McLovin must act mystifying and references the enigmatic nature of the eighth sign of the zodiac.

Returning to the house party, Seth dances with an arbitrary temptress of the hydrous type. **The Ordeal** has emerged, unbuttoning the collar of unexpected circumstances and receiving the nuances of the unknown.

After Seth engages in a private dance moment, the truth bubbles to the surface, and it is revealed that Seth's pants have a bloodstain, displaying the crimson eye of Pluto. Seth understands the idea of exactitude due to a side character pointing it out.

Seth then enters the basement of the house party or the inner sanctuary of his subconscious mind. There he finds a treasure — liquor in the refrigerator.

The lunar hero Evan planned to flee during the Libra stage but must call his consort Becca. He is compelled back into the belly of the beast since no phone service is available outside. Evan searches a private room for a phone. He assures Becca that he is still going to Jule's party, "*Full Throttle, Charlie's Angels 2,*" and indicates a tendency for the hero in Scorpio to charge headlong into every circumstance.

Several older gentlemen enter the room where Evan is without warning and abruptly interrupt his phone call. The hero politely transforms into a "nobody" and nothing, and the previous ego construct is slightly shattered.

Seth attempts to leave after emerging from the bellows with the golden key. Unexpectedly stopping him is the homeowner Mark, and Scorpio's shadow aspect shows how decisions have consequences. They both have blood stains on their thighs, which Mark points out to Seth after revealing that the person he was dancing with earlier was his fiancee.

The party's many groups start to quarrel with one another, which draws attention to the rising tension. The disruption grows as the characters mix and engage in a free-for-all battle royal. The solar and lunar heroes reunite, successfully escaping Scorpio's hidden crevices as they run out of the party.

Trainspotting

Renton looms on a big cement wall outside the pub as the Scorpio era and **The Ordeal** emerge. One of the best transitions in the film shows him leaping off the wall and landing inside Swanney's house, also known as "Mother Superior," the home of his dealer and the Scorpio archetype of the film.

Renton has returned to his shameless ways after embracing his forbidden side. His ethical code has changed due to his fronting of honest sincerity. Renton takes another hit and nearly bites the dust. He enters the chasms of the unconscious abyss in a surrealistic dive into the carpet.

Swanney leads Renton out to the street while remaining composed and sincere. Renton is, after all, a true friend. After returning Renton's money to his breast pocket, Swanney dispatches him in a taxi. Invoking assistance from a higher power will come to fruition as the hero will soon enter the next sign of Sagittarius.

Mean Girls

Cady's quality of living dies out symbolically as the Scorpio stage commences. **The Ordeal** begins when Aaron leaves the party, and Janis and Damian appear outside her house. Janis explodes with the objective reality of the situation and reveals Cady's transformation into a Plastic in all its sincere honesty.

Cady has become the sum of everything Janis despises and has floated too far into the deep end. Damian and Janis drive off after hurling a painted portrait at Cady. The three of them are shown in the painting smiling sweetly. This dramatically stings the hero and makes her realize what she has been fighting for.

Since Mars, the martial luminary coordinates Aries and Scorpio; Regina is particularly formidable during this stage. Regina creates a page in The Burn Book to engage in cruel retribution. She calls Cady several insulting phrases but turns the quip back on herself by placing her picture there instead. The martial archetype is a powerful user of Scorpio's expertise of going inward and drawing out impurities to leverage a personal advantage.

The Burn Book is subsequently revealed to Mr. Duvall by Regina, who executes a master plan to blame Cady and the other Plastics for the book's existence. As **The Ordeal** comes to a close, Regina distributes fliers with pages from The Burn Book around the school's hallways. With exposure to light, shadows cease to exist. The school erupts in mass hysteria as Regina makes the skeletons in the closet visible for all to see.

Snatch

When Brick Top enters Solomon's pawnshop, he delivers a speech in which he refers to the fact that he is the Leo archetype's archenemy. He is instilling fear into them for robbing his bookies. In keeping with the themes of **The Ordeal,** which deals with the concept of death and decay, Brick Top instructs the group on how to dispose of a body by slicing it into pieces and feeding it to pigs at a pig farm.

Avi and Doug are seated at a bar without knowing the whereabouts of the diamond. Doug accurately tells Avi that he is not a bounty hunter capable of tracking down who has the diamond. Bullet Tooth Tony, a Scorpio personification, is introduced in a cut-away scene. The film flashes back to Bullet Tooth Tony getting shot six times in a row and surviving in a narration by Doug The Head. Tony is a person who has gone through death and emerged on the other side stronger than before.

Brick Top and his crew take Sol, Vinny, and Tyrone captive in their pawnshop. Brick Top has positioned plastic everywhere to press the Leo's permanently. Solomon buys more time by asking Brick Top for three days to deliver the diamond in exchange for allowing them to live. Brick Top agrees to the proposal since the shady side desires a taste of the brilliant Sun.

9

— • —

SAGITTARIUS - SEIZING THE SWORD

After the brief destruction, the heroes seize a symbolic or literal sword of a new day. In the last stage of the second act, the heroes start the retreat out of the **Special World** and reach the ninth stage, **Seizing the Sword**.

Sagittarius is elevated foresight and swayed by a code of belief and conviction in a universal life form. Mutable fire connects to lively animation dispersed like an arrow shot at a target. It is stated that having trust, rather than accuracy, is the finest method to shoot an arrow.

Propelled toward a new light at the end of the Scorpio tunnel, the heroes show their next move in response to an increased provocation. After dealing with the effects of a significant choice, they must now decide where to aim next.

The luminary with the most significant size Jupiter, the ruler of Sagittarius, intervenes to provide upbeat energy that offers hope to those who have lost their way. The sign of the archer corresponds to the god of thunder, Zeus, from Greek mythology, and Thor, from Norse mythology. Zeus and Thor are emblematic of Jupiter and are identified as controlling a lightning bolt. Sagittarius adds a connection to a more significant source of intangible stimulus.

The heroes will trust an invisible force that ignites an action-oriented goal, soaring after a spiritual fire as the lower nature is extinguished by striving for the heavenly realms.

Star Wars: A New Hope

Opening the ninth stage of **Seizing the Sword**, Obi-Wan and Darth Vader engage in a lightsaber duel as the two forces of the galaxy clash. This particular hero's quest appropriately emphasizes and displays the use of a saber made of light.

Ultimately, an unrestrained spirit is more potent than temporal flesh and blood. This idea is demonstrated when Obi-Wan suggests to Vader during the fight that if he loses, he will return more vital than anybody could comprehend.

Obi-Wan deliberately loses and engages in a sacrifice to aid Luke and the others in escaping. Luke witnesses this, forcing the hero to put more faith in his powers. The leading role can no longer rely on the mentor's advice and support.

Numerous well-known stories use this troupe, including *The Lord of the Rings*. Gandalf purposely leaves Frodo and the fellowship after almost defeating the "Balrog." The sacred situation compels the hero to trust in a more significant motivation.

There is typically a chase scene that enhances mobility inside the agility of malleable fire. The antagonists try to slow the swiftly moving hero down. The crew prepares to leave as the Empire closes in, and they barely manage to take off in the Millenium Falcon.

Han and Luke then combat Imperial Ti-fighters in the gun turrets, demonstrating the idea of putting one's faith to the test through action. Luke discovers how to harness the power within and eliminates the imperilment as the Falcon soars into hyper-speed.

Leia states that the Imperial forces let them escape on purpose. Since R2-D2 has the Death Star's technical workings, the Empire is still actively pursuing them. Leia affirms that the Empire is not yet ready to wipe them out.

More information is provided regarding the Rebel Alliance's revolution. Jupiter presents a fighting chance in Sagittarius, pushing back against Saturn's tangible limitations in the physical realm. The Princess exemplifies the value of trust. Faith must be directed toward a new goal in any revolution. Due to their conversation, Leia eventually suggests to Han Solo that he must prioritize something other than his gain.

Fear and Loathing in Las Vegas

After probing the depths of the subconscious state, the Sagittarius cycle takes shape the following morning in the hotel room. The rays of sunshine brutally beam in, and a loud zap welcomes Hunter back to the land of the living. Jupiter packages a sharp sensation like a lightning bolt as the bellhop rings the door buzzer.

The film clarifies that Gonzo has been relocated, and Hunter is trying to figure out what to do next. This moment allows him to move along a more comprehensive pathway. Sagittarius maintains a fiery disposition and spurs the hero to action as he is forced to put his confidence into the unknowable. He frantically packs the car and dashes out of the destroyed hotel room.

Outside the hotel, the clerk stops Hunter before he can drive off. The Mint Hotel clerk acts as a barrier for the hero. A discussion about a lunch date follows, and a sense of urgency permeates the setting. Hunter states that he needs to partake in the race. The clerk responds, saying that the race is over. Not according to Hunter! The hero exits the **Special World** of Las Vegas with forward momentum.

As the solar hero drives off into the Nevada desert, a highway cop, played by Gary Busey, starts to chase him. The hot pursuit is on! With nowhere else to turn, Thompson prays to God for a few more hours of freedom. The officer stops Hunter but is unable to constrain the Sagittarius fire. The hero continues his travels through the desert.

Due to his desire to flee, Hunter winds up ashtray at the edge of the Barstow desert. He calls Dr. Gonzo from a phone booth as he searches for help from beyond. Gonzo offers him a shot of redemption and tells Hunter to return to Las Vegas since he has secured a new hotel room at "The Flamingo Hotel."

The film cuts to Thompson shooting a hand cannon in the desert while narrating a wise saying. He says that the giant magnet's whims determine how energy flows. One will be steered off course if one ignores the enormous pull of faith in the unknown.

Superbad

Seth and Evan seize the sword by escaping the party's conflict and prepare to exit the **Special World** as the point of Sagittarius manifests. As the heroes gallop through the neighborhood, McLovin and the police accidentally and suddenly strike them with the squad car. The social norms of the material world briefly counteract the forward velocity while both storylines converge.

Seth and Evan's faith is tested as they lay belly-first on the pavement. The cops are preparing to blame them for the entire incident as a slow-motion scene develops in preparation for arrest. However, Evan portrays mutable fire and swiftly dashes away from the cops at top speed. The implied chase scene picks up!

Evan successfully outruns Officer Michaels and wins his freedom. Evan has the spirit of hope in him. McLovin and Seth escape their bonds, and the three leading roles reassemble to prepare for their departure from the second act.

In closing the Sagittarius segment, the three board a bus to travel to Jule's party. They stumble into the perp the police had caught and released earlier. The vagrant struggles with Seth while attempting to steal some of their alcohol. The "Goldslick Vodka" shatters as it falls onto the bus floor. Visually, this represents mutable, everchanging fire bursting out in several directions. As a result, Evan will be inspired to believe in himself and behave with more chivalry.

Trainspotting

The Sagittarius chapter begins in *Trainspotting* as Renton is rescued from the street. He is taken to the hospital, and a defibrillator uses a bolt of Sagittarius energy to jump-start the hero back to life.

Leaving the **Special World**, Renton's parents keep him safe and serve as guardian angels, trying to help guide him to get better. Trust and faith authorize a transition into a revitalized sense of life.

Ironically, Renton cannot project himself in all directions, which is the Sagittarius hero's impulse. A psychotropic rehabilitation scene appears as he is forced into recovery. Renton is under pressure to atone for his previous actions. Atonement is a connection to one's higher self. The tension is dialed up, and the hero is internally restored.

When Mark Renton is born again, Diane makes a brief cameo, and they resume their relationship. She tells him that he must find something new to do and seize the sword of a new day since time is a finite resource, and everything must move on. This officially leads the hero out of the **Special World** and ignites his enthusiasm and strength to continue.

Mean Girls

As soon as Mr. Duvall, the voice of reason, tells the junior ladies to head straight to the gymnasium, the Sagittarius stage occurs. The celestial male figure administers a communal push out of the shadows. The hero in **Seizing the Sword** must endure a symbolic "trial by fire." This forges drastically with the divine flow of energy to unite the lower and higher natures within the dual framework of reality.

As the film cuts to the gymnasium, Mr. Duvall says these teenagers must change their attitudes. As only one-half of spiritually inclined divinity, Mr. Duvall requires Ms. Norbury to complete him in this endeavor. She assumes her proper role and moves forward to help them all change their collective perspective.

Exercises for the feminine to verbalize anger in healthy ways are brought to pass by Ms. Norbury. Everyone airs their dirty linen and submits to unexpected joy by formulating trust with literal trust falls.

In her testimony before the audience, Janis admits to using Cady as a conduit to destroy Regina. The crowd applauds Janis when she makes a heartfelt confession. Regina unceremoniously exits the gymnasium, and Cady follows her to correct her mistakes.

As the two opposing personalities briefly square off outdoors, Cady tries to shed some light on the matter. Regina experiences firsthand the broad side of a bus as the situation is quickly resolved with a higher authority having the ultimate word and the situation getting the decisions of a hat trick settled.

Snatch

Bullet Tooth Tony and Avi set out on a hunt. They seek to identify the perpetrators who robbed the bookies, thus revealing the location of the diamond. They visit Solomon's pawnshop, and Sol informs Tony and Avi that Boris has the diamond. Since Tony knows Boris The Blade's notoriety, he refers to him as "Boris The Bullet Dodger." This nickname denotes Sagittarius' capacity to effortlessly sidestep and avoid dangers by connecting to changeable fire and harnessing Jupiter's greater source strength. Avi and Tony eventually obtain the diamond after painstakingly capturing Boris.

A montage vehicle scene involves three storylines: Turkish and Tommy, Sol and Vinny, and Avi and Tony. This scene refers to the mobility shown during this portion of the journey. The vehicle sequence alternates between the three different cars. Framing Sagittarius themes, Tommy refers to his universal philosophy and shares his perspective with Turkish on the drawbacks of drinking milk.

Avi's bodyguard Rosebud describes how he will use a knife to take out Boris, who is situated in the car's boot. The knife, according to Tony, is inadequate, and he indicates that he has a larger blade. The actual sword Tony refers to is the appropriate size and refers to this part of the voyage as the heroes learn to seize the sword.

Eventually, the car montage builds to a crescendo when the cars collide. This enables Boris to escape since he embodies relentless forward momentum. After the sideswipe and the dash against one another, Avi and Tony still own the diamond. They seek safety at a nearby tavern.

In the following scene inside the tavern, Vinny and Sol attempt to reclaim the diamond from Tony. However, they submit to Tony's

"Desert Eagle .50" monologue, which portrays the possibility of unquenchable gunfire.

When Boris arrives brandishing a machine gun, chaos ensues. A standoff incident occurs in the tavern's corridor between the characters. Only Boris is struck when Tony fires his Desert Eagle through the wall. Before they can get away, Sol and Vinny take the suitcase containing the diamond. The Leo archetypes are given a ray of optimism.

Turkish informs Brick Top that Mickey will only compete in the next rigged match once they purchase a larger caravan for Mum O'Neil. Brick Top uses forward velocity to persuade his adversaries aggressively. He sends his goons to destroy Turkish's arcade. The movie depicts an aerial shot looking down on Turkish as he is moments away from being hacked by one of Brick Top's henchmen, who is brandishing a blade. Turkish is shown being almost sliced on the cross in a shot that relates to Sagittarius' connection to Jupiter and the idea of yielding to a greater force.

Tommy then steps in to save the day, musters up divine courage, and shows off his character growth as he seizes the initiative by changing the balance of power. Tommy is ready to fire if they try to inflict any more destruction. The hero archetypes manage to get away.

Brick Top then sends his men to set fire to Mickey's mum's caravan. This scene in the film depicts a significant meta-symbolic moment. Brad Pitt, whose Sun and Rising sign is Sagittarius. He is as Sagittarius as they come, with fire enveloping his face. Mickey feels additionally compelled at this time to embrace the need to take on a higher calling.

10

— . —

CAPRICORN - THE ROAD BACK

The hero is pledging to make the long ascent up the steep slope while sailing the ship of a new duty. **The Road Back** refers to the hero's symbolic movement up the proverbial mountain. Capricorn themes embody the Sun's yearly trek back to its precursory state from the Nothern Hemisphere's lowest point and an inner sense of establishment firmly rooted in the outside world.

The third act begins by encouraging the hero to build upon the forward momentum activated in the Sagittarius phase. The internal fire must be kept alive despite the sky's faint illumination. Capricorn energy suggests a sense of status, jumping over obstacles to achieve goals and building directly on top of previous achievements. The vibrant Sagittarius spirit is grounded in earthly reality by the final cardinal sign.

The environment is bone-chillingly cold during the Capricorn season and most of the Northern Hemisphere. Only a tiny fraction of the day is spent with the Sun visible in the sky, proving that palpable solid reality is more noticeable; the force of the sunshine is indisputably constrained.

The cardinal earth energy, which is magnetic and feminine, enables the hero to initiate physical construction that arises from an internal emotional state. A sea-goat symbolizes this stage since Capricorn's energy helps build and climb in the physical world through inner emotional release, represented by the goat's half-aquatic watery appearance.

The formidable taskmaster, Saturn, the "Lord of the Ring," rules this final earth sign. Capricorn's essence is logically realistic to the notion of practicality and is aware of the structural constraint of the physical world. Saturn is the master of time and is often called "The Grim Reaper." The legend of the "Death Eater" emphasizes the truth that time destroys everything.

Star Wars: A New Hope

The protagonist first displays traits of a goal-oriented achiever at the beginning of **The Road Back**. During a conference at the Rebel base, the Rebel Alliance presents a strategy for attacking the Death Star. This is the application of intuition. A plan is developed to exploit a slight opening in the Death Star's defenses.

In the following scene, Luke prepares to fly in the attack and assumes Capricorn's reliable manner. Han Solo and Luke engage in a conversation. Han explains his strategy for leaving once he fulfills his end of the contract. He conveys Capricorn's practical preference for the end of the line.

Fear and Loathing in Las Vegas

Beginning the third act with a redesigned architectural framework, **The Road Back** crystallizes as Hunter Thompson returns to Las Vegas in a brand-new white Cadillac Eldorado.

"The District Attorneys Conference on Narcotics" occurs as Hunter enters The Flamingo Hotel. He intends to cover this conference under the influence of a new calling in keeping with Saturn's preference for legal and orderly systems. The hero directs his might more beneficially.

When Hunter arrives at the hotel to check in, a scene representing power dynamics follows the propensity to demonstrate structural order. A police chief from Michigan who holds the title of a position of superior authority is on the late list. Unquestionably Capricorn personified, this character then starts a commotion in the lobby. His reservation is moved to another hotel, and he openly lashes out at the clerk.

A scenario in Hunter's imagination shows a scene in which the clerk recognizes the true source of authority and correctly condemns the police chief. This instance demonstrates an aptitude for communicating the reality of power relations.

Hunter enters his new hotel room, where Dr. Gonzo and Lucy, a Capricorn-oriented character, greet him. She is a painter who filled the hotel room with a sizable collection of Barbra Streisand paintings. The aesthetic integrity of Capricorn brings about the development of material form.

Superbad

At the entrance of Jules' party, Seth, Evan, and McLovin are preparing to embark on **The Road Back**. But before they enter, Saturn stops them with a feasible fist. Seth learns from McLovin that he and Evan will share a room at Dartmouth the following year. As the reality of the situation sets in, McLovin behaves capriciously and does not feel sorry for Seth. The hero understands that he must scale a higher emotional hill to become more assertive on the other side.

There is a sense of importance and a capacity for adopting the objective as the three leads enter the party. With such vigor, the heroes have navigated the journey's spiral staircase. They have established a reputation for themselves and have upheld the value of perseverance. The celebration erupts in ravished delight at Seth's arrival.

Each of the three leads experiences a love scene. McLovin, who represents Capricorn's desire for increased status, reaches his capstone as a big kahuna of notoriety, approaching his love interest with assurance by dancing with her.

Evan's laurels afford him the affection he yearned for from Becca, and she drunkenly desires him. Upholding Capricorn's code of morality and reputable character, Evan also gets inebriated to remain ethical. Seth understands the unreserved fact that Jules doesn't drink and will not partake in any sexual activity with him as he is intoxicated.

While Seth and Evan share personal moments with their female partners, their relationships do not end in promiscuity. In contrast, McLovin embraces his evolved trait of prestige and succeeds when he loses his virginity. The three become entangled in their different positions of rank.

Trainspotting

For his entry into the Capricorn era, Renton is sanctified with a greater sense of personal legitimacy. After arriving in London, he settles into a new home and career as a real estate agent. Saturn and the structural earth sign are related to this new and improved status for the hero.

The film depicts Renton working hard to achieve both material and financial success. He weaves a line of narration that implies the capacity to make money amid complete pandemonium. During the Capricorn stage, the hero is becoming a conscientious externalization of time, which equates to money. Renton implies in the narration that for the first time in his adult life, he is almost content, alluding to Saturn's strong emphasis on responsibly maturing.

The film cuts to a sequence as Renton reads a letter from Diane. She narrates that Sick Boy asked her to work for him; Spud is portrayed with an ear-to-the-ground posture in a gutter, and Saturn's law is trailing Begbie for an attempted robbery, among other things.

All of the characters exhibit Capricorn traits and the unquestionable requirement for order within the boundaries of physical reality. As the collective will soon arrive and usher in the Aquarius stage, the goat's presence on the mountaintop is only transitory.

Mean Girls

Beginning in Capricorn, Cady's parents are distraught by their daughter's actions. Cady then converses with her father, who plays a Capricorn expression as someone who holds authority over the hero. He calls her a "lion" and sprinkles her with ambition and fatherly advice. The ascent is the only renewal that follows the symbolic death in Scorpio and the atonement in Sagittarius.

The hero must ascend this steep slope with her head held high while maintaining a tenuous connection to the original spark of light. Cady is "grounded" by imposing Saturn's outer limits and using the proper terminology. Feminine and magnetic energy is firmly and profoundly entrenched in the material plane in all the earth signs of the zodiac.

The film then shifts to Cady at school, where her reputation has worsened. She is again secluded alone in the bathroom stall, her lowest point. She will soon be inspired to return from the foundational summit.

The following scene shows Ms. Norbury being sentenced to the third degree by the police for drug peddling. Cady accepts her inevitable fate and realizes what she must do; she admits to writing The Burn Book and assumes full responsibility. The hero feels motivated to make the journey home after being vindicated. An extra effort must be made for the Sun to be revived again. Ms. Norbury advances that Cady must join "The Mathletes" to receive additional credit.

Snatch

Saturn's outer reaches draw closer to our heroes as they start the Capricorn stage and **The Road Back**. Sol and Vinny are inside their automobile before presenting the diamond to Brick Top, but they are interrupted by Bullet Tooth Tony's unexpected arrival. They inform him the diamond is back at the pawn store.

Cut to Sol and Vinny acting like they are still determining the location of the diamond in the shop. They claim the dog ate it, prompting Tony to draw his gun and almost shoot the canine. However, Vinny reveals the diamond from inside his jeans. He hands it over to Avi, but the dog snatches the diamond moments later. This represents the Sun as it enters Capricorn and is drawn into the physical world of conscious awareness and material design.

As the dog successfully escapes the pawnshop, Avi shoots his gun, accidentally hitting Tony. Avi is rocked hard by the brutal reality that suddenly makes an appearance. Avi is then seen hurriedly flying out of London and back to New York City. For Sol and Vinny, losing the diamond now necessitates a challenging ascent.

The night before the rigged match, Turkish and Tommy reach the end of the line and discuss their worries. In a discussion that unfolds, Mickey is shown to be sufficiently inebriated at the wake of his mother. The film cuts to Mickey, Tommy, and Turkish preparing for the rigged fight the following day. When the hangover sets in, Mickey is cruelly and honestly reminded that he is a human with a purpose to fulfill in the physical world.

11

AQUARIUS - THE RESURRECTION

Welcome to the land of milk and honey. The key participants must decide how to put their new foundations to use on a universal scale by building a framework inside the observable world. What novel approaches might they re-imagine to disrupt the status quo?

The collective awareness is represented by the characters who appear on the scene, and a sense of obligation to the entire community is demonstrated. The themes of the Aquarius stage celebrate imaginative future-focused thinking and active participation in the vast social networks.

The Resurrection represents the quest's zenith and conveys one more climatic call for the hero to pave the road on a grand scale so that others may profit from the trials and tribulations of the journey.

In Aquarius, the hero leads a communal finale pertaining to the fate of the community they are a member of. The hero's intellect and soul are ultimately where the final reawakening occurs.

Fixed air communicates mental awareness by combining all of the various components of mental cognition inside a limited structural framework for progressive evolution. The essential toolkit for forwarding innovation is thought patterns. Unknown brainstorming methods are generated within the dual spectrum of the conscious and subconscious mind.

The human pouring water from a jug is the Aquarius glyph. Jars or pots serve as containers for water and represent the spirit of Aquarius, which creates the shape from which water (purification) will flow in service to the collective.

While providing a pressure release valve, Uranus gives Saturn's steadfastness of purpose a fresh perspective. Saturn will inevitably contain Uranus' quirkiness while displaying an inclination for a higher standard of reality. Finely honed infrastructures for stewardship are in place, yet they are stitched together with an eccentric, outlandish flair.

Star Wars: A New Hope

The Resurrection is in progress as the decisive final battle commences. The radical Rebels embark on a humanitarian mission. A network is built with a revolutionary alignment to Uranus while inclined to Saturn's ordinance. The Rebel fleet is given numbers, and Luke is identified as "Red 5." The Sun, the fifth sign of the zodiac and a crimson, electric energy, is represented by Luke as the prime example of the Sun.

The small fleet of Rebels progressively advances but suffers losses as the space fight surrounding the Death Star continues. Luke is the sole surviving Rebel pilot, and hope gradually dims as the Empire draws in.

At the very last second, Han Solo makes an incredible comeback and saves Luke from a Ti-Fighter piloted by Darth Vader. Luke uses his mental skills to avoid approaching disaster while bearing the weight of the Rebel Alliance on his shoulders.

Obi-Wan telepathically communicates with Luke and quotes the Force's connection to the Jedi. Luke lets his freak flag fly! He uses his unique skills and talents to benefit the group, strikes his target, and destroys the Death Star.

Fear and Loathing in Las Vegas

Hunter and Dr. Gonzo experience **The Resurrection** in a conference room full of people attending a seminar about alleged drug misuse among young people in 1960s America. This points to an Aquarius theme of upholding the necessity of maintaining social peace. A dope fiend's mentality can be divided into four groups, according to the speaker at the podium, as he describes someone's personality while residing inside the boundaries of a group context using a particular set of vocabulary.

Hunter and Gonzo, the rebellious weirdos of the freak realm, come into focus. They are opposite to what is being discussed in the seminar. Dr. Gonzo yields to the seminar's pomposity and departs rebelliously.

When the film returns to the hotel room, Lucy, who had earlier departed, calls Gonzo. He uses the phone to demonstrate how the element of fixed air interacts using intense focused communication.

Gonzo bursts into a purported act of restrained insanity as he noisily convinces Lucy that he is being attacked so that she won't be a burden to the heroes for the remainder of this voyage.

Following the phone conversation, Hunter and Gonzo engage in an even more brutally unrelenting trip-out sequence. The further reaches of reason are fathomed upon yet are gradually drawn back in by the power of Saturn. Richard Nixon's face is surrealistically spilling out of the television set in a loop to denote the outer authority of Saturn's bounds.

Superbad

The Aquarius stage begins as the police break up Jule's party. The law shows up, causing everyone to run and disassemble; fixed air orchestrates wind confinement like a tornado. Officer Slater dances amid the chaos to demonstrate how Uranus and Saturn are related. This is a visual oxymoron of a police officer acting like one of those rowdy youngsters while refusing to perform his official duties.

While McLovin is losing his virginity in the upper bedroom, the two cops storm in. Officer Michaels said they should guide their young comrade and not prevent him from having his first sexual encounter. The most benevolent interpretation of Saturn's influence describes it as less authoritarian and more of a mentor. Slater and Michaels admit to McLovin that they were aware of his fraudulent identification the entire time.

The police assert that they recognized a little of themselves in McLovin, giving concrete form to Aquarius' philosophy of universal fellowship and seeing oneself in others. They wanted to demonstrate to McLovin that they could enjoy life, if only for themselves.

Evan is shown slumped on the couch; he has consumed too much alcohol and cannot leave the house alone. Seth begins to carry Evan and convoy him out of the party as the dismantling intensifies. Related to **The Resurrection**, the hero is carrying that load and revealing how he is not selfish, like the glyph of the water bearer lifting a jug of water and spilling it out to serve others.

The cops agree to do McLovin one last favor. McLovin incorporates his wild side by leaving the party in cuffs like a legendary rebel. In the following scene, the cops and McLovin burn the squad car in a vacant parking lot. This is another visual rendition of how law enforcement and spontaneous destruction coexist.

Trainspotting

The eleventh phase takes flight when Begbie reappears and starts living with Renton. The hero cannot escape the collective consciousness. Begbie is pleased to have a location to retreat from Saturn's limitations. The film cuts to the two at a nightclub.

As he observes the other club patrons, Renton remarks in voice-over how society is evolving and predicts that everyone will eventually become hive mind-orientated. Perhaps something that is being fought against in the Aquarian age. Begbie mistakenly has sexual relations outside the club with a transvestite and showcases universal acceptance of different creeds, even if unintentional. As the film transitions, Sick Boy reappears for the collective air sign. Sick Boy moves in with Renton and Begbie, and the three begin sharing Renton's small studio flat.

As Sick Boy sells Renton's television set, he illustrates how Aquarius and technological developments are related. A machine is a physical device with numerous moving components, which connects to the idea of disparate parts functioning harmoniously. Additionally, Sick Boy suggests generating money by selling passports and talks about how everyone is simply a cog in the machine.

After the death of Tommy occurs, Spud also reappears in the movie. The four take on the role of water bearers in a *Trainspotting* way. They proceed to complete one more drug sale for a sizable payout and embrace the glyph of Aquarius, in which the water is interpreted as heroin being distributed on a mass scale.

In this stage, the hero's history returns for one last hurrah, and Renton encounters **The Resurrection**. Renton tests a small amount of the new supply since he is the only clean one in the group.

Mean Girls

The Aquarius division unfolds with a montage of the notable characters preparing for the Spring Fling. The film then cuts to Cady, who is still on house arrest. In defiance of authority, she chooses to participate in the math competition. She spontaneously evolves in an orthodox manner. Her resistance to submitting to power and the structural integrity of Saturn is at work as she engages in **The Resurrection**.

The hero soon accepts social differences at the math tournament's grand championship and leans toward group unity. Caroline Craft is the opponent Cady must confront. Cady narrates how condemning Caroline for superficial things won't assist her in math and makes a point about appreciating and recognizing other people as individuals like her.

Caroline answers the question wrong, and circumstances now rest on the hero's shoulders. According to Cady, she relays another Aquarius theme in narration. She remarks that all one can do is try to understand the issue in front of them. She responds by saying, ultimately, the limitation cannot prevail. That is the definitive solution to the problem, and Cady triumphs.

There is a belief that a ceiling does not exist in Aquarius. Saturn established shape during Capricorn, and now that Aquarius comprehends that idea, there is psychological integration to think outside the box. There are no obstacles while formulating the power of the mind through mental enlightenment.

Snatch

The bare-knuckle boxing match that serves as *Snatch's* climax is a perfect example of the anarchy that can be controlled within a square ring. The plan is for Mickey to succumb in the fourth, or our heroes will all cross the great divide at the hands of Brick Top.

Before the fight, Brick Top warns Mickey that if he doesn't perform well, he'll have to put out the fires on the kids' backs at the gypsy campsite. Mickey is currently fighting not just for himself but also for the group and next of kin.

Thought is kept inside the bounds of the physical world by fixed air. This contrived bare-knuckle match is physically demanding but even more so mentally. Mickey performs a watered-down simulation of a fight which is a grueling feat. The Irish gypsy will ultimately determine the outcome as everything rests on his shoulders. Mickey attempts to last until the fourth round while the fight theatrically proceeds.

During a pause in the melee, Turkish aggressively reminds Mickey not to knock the opponent out. The Irish pikey tries his best to make his actions seem credible, which is quite an absurd proposition that makes your head spin. A visual representation of the baptism of Aquarius utilizing water is caused by Tommy pouring water on Mickey's face.

Mickey executes an act of sheer defiance by knocking out his opponent cold in the final split-second of the fourth round. He gambled on himself to win in the fourth rather than follow the plan—a rebellious Aquarius move. Mickey exemplifies the concept of thinking creatively and is intellectually ahead of everyone else. The pikey outsmarted his adversary and performed mentally more skillfully.

At the gypsy campsite, Brick Top's men are being bombarded with bullets by the other pikeys. A brief phone conversation that alludes to the element of air unfolds. When Brick Top calls one of his men, a pikey answers the phone and mentions Brick Top should raise his voice. This can be seen holding a dual meaning as Brick Top should have elevated his thinking to a higher vantage point, just as the pikeys did.

Before Brick Top can reach the heroes, more pikeys are waiting outside the boxing match and take out this underbelly antagonist. Turkish and Tommy are left behind as Mickey drives off after pulling the ultimate resurrection.

12

—·—

PISCES - RETURN WITH THE ELIXIR

Return With the Elixir proposes the final stage will always return to the beginning. However, everything is different. There is recognition of how, in the end, this finale matters when all is said and done. The twin feet are supervised and governed by Pisces, representing the heroes who carry the burden of the entire narrative behind them. The hero is urged to return to **The Ordinary World** in this last phase as a changed person. But that is not all. Once that return is made and felt, what must happen next? Continue to dream the dream, and you shall see.

The leads have completed the quest and brought about significant, widespread change. Now that a person has had a divine expression, infinite possibilities appear in the sea of consciousness. However, the paradox of the fish is contained within. How does the hero intend to proceed while retaining all they have accomplished? The question becomes: is there even a choice?

This notion immediately makes me think of Frodo's departure from Middle Earth and his lifelong friends at the conclusion of *The Lord of the Rings* trilogy; why does he do it? He must, that's why. Due to his extensive experience, he is out of any other options. Too much has occurred; he seeks something more. The secret to establishing contact with the actual origin of creation is in the assimilation of paradox.

Opposite to Virgo, Pisces places faith in letting go of everything the soul has worked so hard to achieve. However, only one foot can look beyond duality into oneness; the other is still in the physical world. Pisces portrays the paradoxical narrative woven throughout the wheel and inspires one to explore the Buddhist principle of detachment as the twin fishes are separate but always connected. To give up control and put faith in the unknowable through unconditional acceptance and love. A state of dissociation is implanted to overcome and release dependence on such attachments.

Star Wars: A New Hope

After completing the enormous work of restoring some degree of order to the galaxy and giving the Rebel coalition a fighting chance, the heroes are given their elixir in the film's concluding scene. Luke, Han, and Chewbacca enter the location of the coronation. As they pass through the doors, two guards stand there and display the twin fish of Pisces. The heroes **Return With the Elixir** as the most heroic John Williams score plays.

Many Rebel Alliance soldiers and officials are in attendance at the coronation. They move together as a single, coordinated entity. These other warriors have developed a global perspective and treat the significant heroes respectfully. This speaks to Pisces' values of treasuring and loving others without conditions. As one starts to recognize themselves in the other, they act to honor and appreciate them.

There is no verbal dialogue in this sequence, only facial gestures. No words are necessary, only feelings. Words, in a way, become meaningless in the deep psychic and spiritually based twelfth sign. Mutable water linked to myriad emotions has an indescribable essence, bypassing language and sending messages through eye contact.

Princess Leia is the one who awards the medals of honor to the heroes. This is very fitting as she is the Divine Feminine archetype. She is dressed entirely in white, displaying the magnetic feminine polarity's purity. White light or magnetism are connected, and both give life its form. The world of visible light is produced by white light, which disperses into the hues of the rainbow.

Additionally, a trinity is depicted in the final frames of the film. Luke represents the prodigal son, and Han Solo is the Divine Masculine. Their combined efforts create the world and bring order to the galaxy. The idea of a trinity is put out to respect the divinity of creation.

Fear and Loathing in Las Vegas

Return With the Elixir appears, and Hunter awakens in a demolished hotel room. The walls are covered in unidentifiable splatter, and beneath him is knee-high water throughout the entire hotel room. The idea of time shifts from linear to cyclical in Pisces. Hunter claims in narration that he has taken part in ingesting every mind-altering substance known to man since "1544 A.D." The final sign of the zodiac suggests a tapestry of experiences from different lifetimes and epochs.

Hunter prowls through the murky filth of the swamp to find a tape recorder. This last phase is characterized by ethereal vibrancy. Pisces intermingles other-worldliness and the spirit for higher learning. The hero listens to a tape recorder to try and piece together some details of what transpired. Thompson is learning to make sense of what appears to be senselessness. He makes a patchwork of distinct energies and stitches them together. The film plays back moments from sporadic intervals in the past as Hunter audibly listens to the recordings.

The symbol of Pisces depicts the fish moving in two opposing directions but remaining linked by a silver cord. Thompson is returning to these moments while staying anchored to the Earth plane.

The closing shot shows Hunter Thompson driving off through the Nevada desert to return to the City of Angels after embracing the cluttered chaos of the interrelated parts. He has the elixir: his enthusiasm to continue onward and awareness of reality's duality. Chaos and order always coexist. The idea of being too bizarre to live and exceedingly too unusual to perish is inherently felt by the hero, who recognizes the fish's dual theme.

Superbad

In the final stage, Evan and Seth put down two sleeping bags in Evan's basement. The sleeping bags, red and blue, visually pay homage to the two fish of Pisces and the idea of electricity and magnetism. The heroes open up about their feelings over the voyage they just underwent and verbally express their utmost respect for one another. This suggests that understanding love is the ultimate solution and the highest form of expression in the journey's final stage. The heroes happily fall asleep as friends once more and respect the notion of unconditional love.

The film cuts to the morning, and the heroes feel refreshed to start a new day. Seth and Evan head off to the mall. At the mall, they come across Jules and Becca, which results in one final act of karma. They must compensate for the previous night's mistakes and make amends. There is a sense of a variety of life's circumstances coming to a definitive conclusion in the final sign of the zodiac. They all must surrender to a higher power by believing in letting go.

The final shot is of Jules and Seth departing one way and Evan and Becca eloping in another. Seth and Evan, our two loving heroes, exchange a silent farewell or a "See you later." The two fish of Pisces part ways but will always remain connected.

Trainspotting

The final section begins once the heroin deal is complete, and the four lads catch some rest in a hotel. Since Neptune rules the concept of the vastness of the subconscious mind, the characters exist in the dream world. However, Renton wakes up before the others and makes a substantial decision.

Mark Renton concludes that he must embark on a solo mission. Giving up what the hero once knew is necessary for this final moment. He, therefore, decides to assert ownership of the elixir (the bag of money) and vanish before the others awaken.

Pisces reflects the idea that life is merely a dream, and there is a quality of disappearing into obscurity and giving complete disorientation to those who might witness it. Yet a moment of twin fishes occurs. Spud wakes up as Renton prepares to exit. They exchange a nonverbal farewell, and one gets the impression that Renton and Spud will still be in touch. The film charmingly illustrates when it is revealed that Renton does leave Spud a bit of the cash.

The last image is a close-up of Renton's face as he is on the move holding the elixir obtained from the quest. He narrates how he ultimately chooses himself. The shot congeals into a single blob of dancing colors and loses focus while distorting the lines.

Mean Girls

When Cady shows up at the Spring Fling, the Sun enters its final phase. The nominations are listed by Mr. Duvall, who crowns Cady as queen. The hero obtained the crown during the journey, a clear physical elixir. What she does with it deepens the significance of the concept. Like Sagittarius, Pisces unites to a more significant power source beyond the self.

Cady delivers a speech as she is crowned and notes how everyone looks grandiose. She distributes the crown's fragments to the other well-known personalities—the many pieces of the whole merge into one. The two words "pieces" and "Pisces" are remarkably similar. This is a sentimental reunion and an acceptance of unconditional acclaim.

During the final stage of the quest, the heavenly feminine and masculine unite. Everyone is seen coupled up as they slow dance. Despite all delay, Cady and Aaron share a climactic kiss.

The journey ends the following year with Cady and the other main characters showing off their brand-new way of life as seniors. Cady explains in narration how she underwent this entire experience to understand the fundamentals of being human. The protagonist claims she has learned to "flow," much like the hero and the Sun, through this twelve-step process.

Snatch

Turkish describes how the gypsies' campground had evaporated overnight and disappeared into the midst after they had to bury twelve bodies and leave town. The number twelve is a nod to the twelfth sign. A humorous and pleasant environment is presented that alludes to the ethereal idea of letting go as water slides off one's back. FBI officers casually question Turkish and Tommy at the deserted campsite. Turkish and Tommy escape unharmed and acquire the dog (the elixir with the diamond).

In the closing scene, Turkish describes finding the diamond inside the dog. Unaware, the heroes had the treasure. The elixir is then given over to Doug The Head. The film ends with Avi returning to London and Turkish and Tommy receiving a handsome sum for the plunders found. Roll credits!

13

—·—

ASTRO CONFIGURATIONS OF EACH FILM

A greater understanding of the energy entering and leaving each movie can be obtained by looking at the actor's astrological profile. With each of these films being a cultural phenomenon, the performers are essentially the characters on some level and will always be remembered as these specific archetypes. Inevitably, the aura of each film is influenced by the actors. Each actor's astrological configuration will naturally be weaved into the narrative and expressed on screen.

Star Wars: A New Hope

The three main characters and the film's creator George Lucas each have a strong Venus influence in their birth charts, which lends the astrology of *Star Wars* a Venusian touch. Venus is also exhibited through the puppetry and the intricate artistic elegance used to create the visuals for this grand cinematic universe. *Star Wars*, a highly collaborative project, displays Venus's community energy signature.

Carrie Fischer and Mark Hamil have Libra Sun and Capricorn Rising signs. The personalities of Luke and Leia incorporate the Libra and Capricorn themes. Carrie has a Taurus Moon sign, whereas Mark has a Leo Moon sign. This reveals their mental state and how they utilize the Leo sunlight and Taurus-aligned personal value system.

In Libra, there is a need for balance, and Luke and Leia's conflict between the two sides of the Force is the motif provided for their prominent roles. Each character's fate emphasizes using a dual framework to test their Jedi abilities. This is their primary path.

The route Luke and Leia will follow to regain equilibrium is through their Capricorn Rising sign. Does the association between Capricorn and "Father Time" seem familiar? Darth Vader is the epitome of Saturn. To fulfill their Libra destiny and tip the scales to the side of the Jedi, Luke, and Leia must defeat Darth Vader and navigate the Capricorn energies.

Harrison Ford has a Cancer Sun sign, and his advancement is to embody the qualities of the Sun's highest peak observed in Cancer season. He was born on a new Moon, which doubles the Cancer energy's portrayal of elevated status and relishing the moment. Ford has his rising sign in Libra and shows a balancing dance of opposites that will lead him to the glory of the summer solstice. Han Solo views most circumstances as being in the middle — neither good nor evil, but just right.

George Lucas is a Taurus Sun, Taurus Rising, and Aquarius Moon. This cinematic environment has its roots in the rock-solid George. His Taurus Sun's destiny is to place self-worth within while assuming an attitude of inward stoicism, faith, and patience. His Rising sign, Taurus, guides him and puts him perfectly in alignment with his calling. His Aquarius Moon demonstrates how, on the inside, he embodies *Star Wars'* peculiar "out of this world" lore.

Fear and Loathing in Las Vegas

The astrology of *Fear and Loathing in Las Vegas* is very mutable and elusive. The two main leads, Johnny Depp and Benicio Del Toro, are mutable Sun signs. Johnny is a Gemini, and Benicio is a Pisces. Gemini and Pisces express a fluid energy transmutation, as all the mutable signs do. The themes in the story connect to mind-altering psychedelics and the fluidity of palpable reality when under such conditions. The facts seem to dissolve into a fantastical dream-like state.

Johnny Depp's life path is aligned with Gemini's qualities of juggling duality, the conscious and the subconscious, the soul and the ego. With his impression of Hunter S. Thompson, Depp embodies playing a dual character as Thompson was an actual person. As Thompson is a prolific writer, his poetic narration fuses with the air element. Johnny's rising sign is Leo, so the path he will take to his Gemini destination is through the expressive, theatrical sign of Leo.

This entertaining psychedelic film's director, Terry Gilliam, has a Scorpio Sun, Leo Moon, and Virgo Rising. In his direction of Hunter S. Thompson's book, which relates to the depths of reaching one's psyche by letting go of attachments to the outside world, Gilliam depicts his Scorpio traits.

I recognize the wit and sardonic humor from Gilliam's early days as an actor with *Monty Python*. His comedy enhances his Scorpio aura and demonstrates how humor can lighten harsher or potentially terrifying situations. He strikes a fascinating balance between absurdity and amusement.

Superbad

Superbad is very connected to the Gemini-Sagittarius axis. Expressing themes related to personal philosophy, universal rationality, identity, and hope at the end of the tunnel. Most of the astrological significance of the actors heavily leans in the direction of either Gemini or Sagittarius. Jonah Hill, who plays Seth, has a Sagittarius Sun sign, and Michael Cera, who plays Evan, has a Gemini Sun Sign, showing a balancing act between the opposite signs. Seth is fiery and expressive, and Evan is less reactive and more logical in his approach to life. Christopher Mintz-Plasse and Bill Hader are also both Gemini Sun signs.

The creator of this comedic film Seth Rogen is an exception to the Gemini–Sagittarius axis as he has an Aries Sun sign and a Capricorn Moon. *Superbad* is roughly based on Seth Rogen's life and shows how his Aries Sun sign reflects his unique individuality and the articulation of his persona. Seth's Capricorn Moon also conjuncts Jonah Hill's Rising sign by one degree in Capricorn and is astrologically authentic as Jonah Hill is portraying Rogen as a teenager.

Trainspotting

The two lead actors in *Trainspotting* express a nature related to the energy of Mars. In astrology, Mars is known as the planet of action and is said to represent the ability to fulfill a desire. It is raw energy. The leading role, Renton, is played by Ewan McGregor, who has an Aries Sun sign. Johnny Lee Miller plays Sick Boy, the second lead role with a Scorpio Sun sign. Each character intrinsically expresses Mars as two halves. As the main character, Ewan McGregor is more electric and masculine, and Johnny Lee Miller is more magnetic and feminine as the enigmatic Sick Boy. Scorpio and Aries have contrasting approaches to life and love.

Another interesting note is that Ewan McGregor's Aries Sun is at eighteen degrees of Aries and is directly conjunct to Johnny Lee Miller's Saturn sign. Saturn will always present barriers, boundaries, and challenges, naturally presenting obstacles for the attributes of the bright energy of the Sun. Sick Boy is an antagonist and presents hurdles for Renton throughout the film.

Mean Girls

The creator of *Mean Girls*, Tina Fey, is a Taurus Sun, Libra Moon, and Leo Rising. The main character Cady, played by Lindsay Lohan, has a Cancer Sun sign, a Taurus Moon, and Gemini Rising. There is a connection between the two solar and lunar energies within Tina's Taurus Sun and Lindsay's Taurus Moon. *Mean Girls* presents very Taurus energy showing a thematic overtone of learning to place inner virtue upon oneself. The balancing act of the Sun and Moon of the leading roles shows a dance of the masculine and feminine essence.

Snatch

The director and writer of *Snatch*, Guy Ritchie, is a Virgo Sun and Aries Moon. Most directors intrinsically showcase the workings of their inner world and the themes connected to their ultimate divine will. *Snatch* undoubtedly incorporates themes related to the sign of Virgo and Aries. Guy Ritchie relays his Virgo Sun sign by showing immense attention to detail in the quick edits and the overall dynamic of the interrelated storylines. Ritchie supports themes of his Aries Moon with in-your-face action.

And let's not forget Mr. Brad Pitt; he has a Sagittarius Sun, Capricorn Moon, and Sagittarius Rising. Brad's aura is aligned with Sagittarius as a passionate, joyful essence associated with the optimistic luminary Jupiter. Brad Pitt has a double energy signature of Sagittarius as his wheel of fortune is aligned to the positive energy of Jupiter as he shoots positivity out to the audience.

Pitt's inner world is tied to Capricorn, as he has a down-to-earth, practical way about him. The character Mickey can connect to Sagittarius and Capricorn, as he is a tough-as-nails bare-knuckle boxer who distributes hope. Mickey ultimately saves Turkish and Tommy during the finale.

Joseph Campbell

Joseph Campbell unquestionably made the Hero's Journey extremely understandable and linked many of the associated pieces, albeit probably not the first to find it. Campbell's passion for myth and many cultures is evident in his prying open the doors of legendary tales by weaving a thread that unified the parallels. He has an Aries Sun, Leo Moon, and Libra Rising.

His destiny was connected to Aries as he led and embraced his uniqueness through his Libra Rising sign, as he appreciated many different cultures. His Moon in Leo illustrated the depiction of the hero (Leo) shifting through innumerable faces (the Moon), hence the title of his book, *The Hero With A Thousand Faces*. His Libra Rising was utilized as he was enthralled by an abundance of mythology, demonstrating his admiration for the notion of diversified traditions worldwide.

Joseph Campbell significantly influenced art with his work and unique perspective on the mono-myth. Christopher Vogler, the author of *The Writer's Journey*, was born in 1949, the same year Campbell published *The Hero With A Thousand Faces*, which is another intriguing synchronicity.

14

CONCLUSION - RISE OF TECHNICOLOR

P isces, the hazy, mysterious sign of the zodiac, rules the development of cameras and the production of moving images. Movies exhibit the idea of art mirroring life similarly to how performances on the stage and theatrical productions do. The black-and-white film was a dreamy escape for audience members and added an otherworldly experience. In a way, cinema is akin to a waking dream. Similarly, one can say life is a waking dream, a persistent one.

The transition to Technicolor marked a significant turning point in cinema history and resembled the human eye seeing the physical world through visible light. Audience members witnessed a single monochrome event that quickly transformed into a multicolored one, much like Dorothy in *The Wizard of Oz* as she entered the magical realm of color.

The seven colors of the rainbow enliven the temporal physical world and exist within two unique polarities at either end; at one side is red, and at the other is blue, expressing the idea of duality engraved into the fabric of physical existence. These two color hues are considered opposites, and a wide range of colors exist in between.

The belief that reality, or "Maya," is an illusion was propagated by ancient cultures. Viewing the illusory temporal world through the framework of the color spectrum is linked and epitomized by the rainbow. Since rainbows only show for a limited time before gradually fading away, the rainbow, the range of visible color, is ultimately just an illusion. The world of color is lovely, fascinating, and hypnotizing, yet fleeting.

The cover art for Pink Floyd's album, *"The Dark Side of the Moon,"* represents the color spectrum. On the album cover, a beam of white light passes through a glass prism and separates into the seven primary colors. The rainbow links to white light as the offshoot and is associated with female energy and magnetism. She (magnetism) produces all the colors between red and blue. Similar to the classic fairy tale of *Snow White and the Seven Dwarfs*. But we must remember that it is only a fantasy; it is a rainbow.

Studying the intricacy of the Hero's Journey and the astrological wheel can help you realize your skills and teach you how to use the many moving parts to surpass any predicaments duality throws at you. You can follow your hero's journey by looking at your birth chart and start precisely tracking your journey by following the Sun as it moves through your twelve houses yearly. Begin with the Rising sign, which is **The Ordinary World**. Continue onward from your rising sign until the Sun reaches **Return With the Elixir** in your twelfth house.

Everyone will embark on their personal hero's journey and set out on the route of their divine will. You can find your inner hero and triumph, no matter the challenges and victories along the quest. Everything has led you to this moment to follow the heroic path.

INDEX